SECRET SORROW

SECRET SORROW

GRIEVING AND HEALING
AS A NON-GRANDPARENT
IN A GRANDPARENTING WORLD

MARY ELLEN T. MILLER
PhD, RN, PHNA-BC

ISBN: 978-1-958150-41-2
Secret Sorrow: Grieving and Healing as a Non-Grandparent in a Grandparenting World
First publication: November 2024

Published by **Inner Peace Press**
Eau Claire, Wisconsin, USA
www.innerpeacepress.com

Dedicated to
Phoenix Carson
Forever my treasured first grandchild

Table of Contents

PREFACE

$\mathcal{I}$ am someone who longs to be a grandparent, but, due to my life circumstances, am not a grandparent. I am a non-grandparent.

In my view, a non-grandparent is not merely someone who does not have a grandchild. A non-grandparent is someone who yearns to be a grandparent, yet is not one, and has strong emotional feelings about this elusive milestone.

I used my lived experience as a non-grandparent and my professional experience as a Registered Nurse (RN) to help me convey my grieving and healing as a non-grandparent in writing this book, which I believe is long overdue.

I also wrote this book for you, my non-grandparent companion.

My main takeaway from this book is that the feelings that non-grandparents have are not trivial and are worthy of validation. It is vital that non-grandparents hear my message and learn from my story. It is also crucial for family, friends, and health care professionals of non-grandparents to support non-grandparents on their life journey. My hope for readers who love a non-grandparent is that this book provides some helpful suggestions to be a source of support to the non-grandparents they love.

I believe there are countless non-grandparents among us who keep their feelings about their grief to themselves. My main takeaway is that we are not alone, and we deserve to be supported in our non-grandparent journey.

You may be a non-grandparent because, like me, your child is experiencing infertility or has had a pregnancy loss. There are many, many reasons why someone is a non-grandparent. I discuss these in Chapter 3. However, you may be a non-grandparent for a reason that I didn't think of. If so, I am extremely sorry that I have not included your personal non-grandparent circumstance in my book. I hope you contact me so I can be better informed and include your life circumstances whenever I speak or write about non-grandparents. The more awareness we can have over how we became non-grandparents, I believe it will enable everyone to speak more openly about it, so it no longer has to be secret. We can allow our grief to run its normal course, which is clearly better for our health.

It is vital to note that if an adult child makes a conscious decision not to have a child, their decision needs to be respected by their parent/parents. This is not my non-grandparent experience but it is my belief that having a child is a personal decision that should not be undertaken to meet the expectation of others.

Except for the information in this book about statistics related to infertility, pregnancy loss, grandparenting surveys, and theories of grief, this book is about my personal lived experience as a non-grandparent. Narratives from other non-grandparents are also included to support my beliefs about non-grandparenting sorrow and the huge hesitancy non-grandparents have discussing personal feelings about non-grandparenting with others. I believe I have treated their stories with the reverence they deserve. I truly hope I did.

I welcome feedback from readers. I want non-grandparents to know they are not alone. It is also my hope that non-grandparents no longer keep their grief and sorrow a secret. We deserve to be supported in our life journey.

Mary Ellen
Pocono Pines, PA
October 2024

Introduction

*I*n this book, I give the reader my perspective of what it is like to live as a non-grandparent. I offer suggestions about how non-grandparents can cope with daily life and how family members, friends, and healthcare professionals can support non-grandparents. This is my gift to other non-grandparents and those who love them.

For several years I felt like I was traveling alone in my journey as a non-grandparent. After talking to some other people who also desired to be grandparents but for various reasons were not, I knew this was not just happening to me. I tried to find a book or a pamphlet in my local bookstore that could possibly help me deal with my feelings. I found nothing. I then looked online for any type of publication and struck out there. I realized the book in your hands needed to be written. I believe "Secret Sorrow" needs to be shared with non-grandparents, those who love them, and those who care for them in professional practice.

My early childhood experiences helped shape my perception of how vital a grandparent is to a family. When

I was growing up, my maternal grandfather lived with us. Grandpa was a widower and retired. He moved in with my newlywed parents "temporarily" for cardiac health reasons and remained in their home until he passed away 24 years later. My first experiences with the grandparenting role came from Grandpa. He was actively involved in helping my parents raise six children. He did occasional babysitting, picked us up from school, came to our arts and sporting events, and drove us to places we needed to go when my parents were unable to do so.

Once I married, my parents and my husband's parents were hands-on grandparents. They too interacted with our daughters like my own grandfather did. Because of two pregnancy losses, I was on bedrest during my last two pregnancies. Both sets of grandparents helped us tremendously at this time. For the first bedrest experience we had no children at home. Nonetheless, our parents helped my husband with the normal household chores and also took me to specialist appointments when his work schedule did not permit him to do so. My second pregnancy on bedrest was more challenging because we had a daughter who was a toddler. When my husband was at work, I was unable to do the routine parenting she needed at this time. Her grandparents filled in while my husband worked, primarily to see that her needs were met. In addition to my husband, I have tremendous gratitude to my parents and my in-laws (all of whom are now deceased) for my successful pregnancy outcomes. These lived experiences with grandparents and grandparenting roles helped to shape my mindset of what being a grandparent entails.

My professional background is in nursing. I have over 40 years of experience as a registered nurse working in various specialty areas in healthcare. My early career was in staff nursing. My first staff position was at a community hospital on a medical-surgical unit for a brief three months. As soon as a position became available in the labor and delivery unit, I was filled with anticipation to interview for it. This unit was my original first choice for employment as a graduate nurse. I was elated when I was the candidate selected for this position. A maternal-child nursing role brought me great personal satisfaction. I was fulfilled knowing that I made a difference in the care each of my patients and their families received while pregnant and giving birth. I learned from my seasoned nurse mentors that it was not just a baby, but a family that was born in the delivery room.

After birth, interactions with families included education regarding how to care for the baby. This included care of the umbilical cord, infant bathing, feeding, sleeping patterns, and, most importantly, caring for yourself as a new parent. My nursing education, inpatient experience as a maternal-child nurse, and my personal experience as a mom were all instrumental for me to guide families. I interacted with more than just new moms and dads during my years as a maternal-child nurse – I interacted with siblings, other family members, and grandparents too.

I witnessed interactions that grandparents have with their new grandchildren during this time. I vividly remember new and experienced grandparents holding, feeding, dressing, singing, and talking to their new grandchild. I saw their excitement and joy having a grandchild represent a new generation in the family. Although I was in my 30s at this time, I now believe that I tucked away these life lessons in my mind as grandparenting roles that I would truly want to engage in sometime in the future with my own grandchildren.

Working in a hospital setting was demanding in terms of workload and long hours. Once my children were born, I needed more flexible working hours and I obtained a position as a maternal-child homecare nurse. This position allowed me to work mainly on weekends. I was blessed to interact with families for a longer period of time than just a brief hospitalization. Because I interacted with these families' multiple times, over weeks or months, I truly got to know them and their healthcare needs. My passion as an advocate for families remained with me not only during my career but in my personal life as well. I believe that family health and well-being is the cornerstone of a healthy community, and therefore, a healthy nation.

My employment as a homecare nurse also allowed me to have some flexibility to return to graduate school. When my children were school aged, I earned my master's degree in nursing. I worked as a public health nurse in Philadelphia and began teaching part time at my alma mater. Following this, I taught full time at a university in the Lehigh Valley. I was a nurse educator for over 30 years. During this time, I also earned my PhD in health studies and later became nationally board certified as an Advanced Public Health Nurse. I retired from full time employment in 2016. Until 2023, I directed an interprofessional community health internship for health professions students in Pennsylvania each summer. My years of interactions with students from various disciplines, such as nursing, medicine, and social work, are so very rewarding. Students always teach me new lessons. I learn more from interactions with my students than they ever learn from me.

Based upon my personal and professional life experiences, I embarked upon the journey to write this book for non-grandparents, those who love them and health care professionals who encounter them in various practice settings.

As I began to write my book chapters, I also wrote a couple articles about my lived experience that were published in loss and grief resources. I am beyond grateful to the editors of the online grief resources of *Still Standing Magazine* and *Grief Digest*. My articles about my journey as a non-grandparent due to my daughter and son-in-law's pregnancy loss were published in these sources. When I wrote about my lived experience as a non-grandparent, I initially viewed non-grandparenting through an infertility and pregnancy loss lens. I quickly learned that I had a very narrow focus. Several parents who lost their only child and who now would never be a grandparent contacted me after reading my article published in *Still Standing Magazine*. They pointed out how I had overlooked their pain in my article. To paraphrase, some comments I received were:

"There are thousands of parents who have lost an only child… I speak for them… We have to support each other."

"We often feel misunderstood and isolated. I was a mother but will never be a grandmother."

These quotes are found online at:
https://stillstandingmag.com/2019/07/24/silence-is-not-golden-navigating-non-grandparent-grief/comment-page-3/#comments

I learned so much from non-grandparents who had life experiences that differed from mine! I apologized to each of these parents for my omission of parents who lost an only child in my writing. I promised these grieving parents of only children who died that I would always include them in any future writings on the topic of non-grandparenting. It was never my intent to omit, and therefore, hurt anyone.

If you are someone who desires to be a grandparent but for whatever reason you are a non-grandparent, you may be experiencing feelings of grief and loss. As a nurse, I realize that those who experience **any** type of loss are at risk for depression. This book does not replace the advice of your healthcare professional. Contact your healthcare professional if you need to speak to someone about your feelings. If you are experiencing overwhelming feelings of sadness, or thoughts of harming yourself or others, call 911 or 988, or go to the nearest emergency room.

It did not take me very long to decide on a title for this book. I know that a non-grandparent grieves and that they keep this a secret from others, even their closest friends and family members. I know that a non-grandparent is surrounded by grandparents in every aspect of their life. *Secret Sorrow: Grieving and Healing as a Non-Grandparent in a Grandparenting World* precisely and concisely describes feelings and experiences I carried within me for a very long time, and shares experiences of others I have met along my journey. The title also expresses the key message I convey in this book.

I believe my lived experience healing as a non-grandparent in a grandparenting world needs to be shared to help others know that they are not alone in their journey. Knowing yourself is the first step towards healing.

My main goal for non-grandparents is that you find this book helpful to you in your daily life. I also anticipate that family members, friends, neighbors, co-workers, and healthcare professionals of non-grandparents will also find this information valuable. If I impart some understanding of techniques that helped me cope with my feelings based upon my lived experience and help only one non-grandparent, one person who loves and/or cares for them, or one healthcare professional who encounters a non-grandparent in their practice setting, my goal will have been met. Thank you for making room for this topic in your sphere of interest.

CHAPTER 1

My Ah-ha Moment: My Non-Grandparent Revelation

"Life is what happens to us when we are making other plans." -Allen Saunders

You may wonder: What do you mean by non-grandparent?

I came up with the term "non-grandparent" to provide validation to myself and others by giving a name to someone who deeply desires to be a grandparent but has not experienced this life milestone.

You may be a non-grandparent. Or, you may know and love a non-grandparent or two. I believe there are many non-grandparents hidden among us.

If you are a non-grandparent, my story about healing as a non-grandparent is my gift to you. My story is also my gift to those who know and love a non-grandparent. Equally important, my story is a gift to healthcare professionals who will encounter non-grandparents in their practice settings.

I believe my experience of grieving and healing as a non-grandparent in a grandparenting world needs to be shared. Non-grandparents need to know that they are not alone in their journey.

In 2014, I thought I was going to be a grandparent! My husband and I were filled with joyous anticipation when our daughter and son-in-law announced they were pregnant! Our daughter and son-in-law were going to be parents for the first time! We thought we were going to be grandparents! Instead, we all were taken down a deep abyss for which we were not prepared.

Without warning the pregnancy was over in the eleventh week. We were devastated after spending so much time dreaming of the future with a baby in our family.

I remember only some of the specifics of the time of their miscarriage. I believe it is my mind's way of protecting me even until this day. I remember my daughter's crying voice when she called me late on a Monday evening saying she was bleeding. When my daughter phoned me, my husband and I were sitting in our family room watching the movie *Good Will Hunting* on our television. It took me quite a long time, probably weeks, to sit in the same chair in our family room once again. To this day, when we are looking for a movie on the television and *Good Will Hunting* is playing, I cannot watch it. My husband knows this because I asked him to turn off the TV channel the first time I saw this movie playing again about a month after the miscarriage. To this day he scans past this movie when it is on TV, quickly changing the channel out of respect for my feelings.

I knew my daughter was home alone because her husband worked evenings. I told her I was coming over until he got home, and she sounded relieved to hear me say this. I arrived shortly after my son-in-law did. They both asked me to come with them to the local emergency room. I suspected she was having a miscarriage. I felt like this should be their time alone together but they insisted I come along and I willingly did. It took an exceptionally long time, in the middle of the night, when we heard the devastating news from the ER doctor about the miscarriage. My son-in-law's parents and my husband were texting me frequently during this time in the ER. My daughter asked me to let them all know. When I phoned them, I tried to be strong, but we were all crying. This was everyone's baby.

A lot of that Monday night into Tuesday morning is a blur to me. One thought I do remember during this time was: maybe she was carrying twins and she was losing just one of them. Her ultrasound in the sixth week of her pregnancy did not detect twins. Due to my maternal-child nursing experience, I knew this did happen occasionally. If she was losing one twin this would be so very hard, but they (we) would still have one baby. Of course, this was not reality. It was only my mind's way of coping at the time. I never told them what I was thinking that long, long night.

I know I am blocking out certain memories of the evening and night of the miscarriage to protect myself. And that's ok. I needed to protect myself then. I need to protect myself now.

Cards and flowers were sent to their home. People did all the "right" things to let them know they cared about them. They told me that they could feel the support and the love. They were there for each other. Yet, the days and weeks to come were extremely hard for them. This is how the long and winding road of grief is.

Their pregnancy loss brought back a flood of memories to me. I lost my first two pregnancies. My first pregnancy ended at 26 weeks. I started hemorrhaging during the night because my placenta separated prematurely from my uterus (a placental abruption). Premature labor contractions quickly followed. Our daughter, Marissa, lived for eight days in a Neonatal Intensive Care Unit (NICU). She died from complications of extreme prematurity. My second loss was remarkably like my daughter's. My second pregnancy also resulted in a miscarriage late in the first trimester. Our pregnancy losses were devastating for me and my husband. We too were only in our 20s at the time.

I think it's important to reveal my personal pregnancy stories in this book because my infertility grief came roaring back to me with the loss of my anticipated grandchild. I had tucked away most of my feelings associated with my pregnancy losses. If I allowed myself to, I could replay my losses over the days, weeks, months, and years ahead, following them in my head like a video recording. Over the years, I learned to recognize when I found my mind wandering into my loss experiences, and eventually forced myself to think about something else. I tried, and succeeded, to think about some other life experience that brought me joy. This was my coping mechanism. This is what worked for me in my personal pregnancy grief journey.

It is quite possible that my daughter and son-in-law's pregnancy loss was more devastating for me because of my own pregnancy losses. I could relate to how overwhelming their miscarriage experience was for them. However, I made it clear to them that I did not "know how you feel." No one knows how someone else feels when a loss of any kind happens. I tried to comfort them, too. I gave them a shoulder to lean on. I told them I would be there for them anytime day or night. They knew I was hurting, but didn't know just how much. Their pregnancy loss had to center on them and their dashed hopes and dreams for their first child. They named their baby Phoenix. The Phoenix bird symbolizes renewal, rebirth, and resurrection.

After the miscarriage, for several Mondays in a row, I would think about "that Monday." That Monday started out as such a regular day and ended with such profound sadness. Because I had unexpected pregnancy losses, the lyrics to this song were a stark reminder to me about how each day when we wake up, we do not know what is in store for us that day. Anything, good or bad, happy or sad, could happen to us. Some months later, just as I felt as if I was getting back to normal (whatever that really is), I heard an old song from the 1960s on the car radio as I was driving home from work. The song was "Monday, Monday" by the Mamas and the Papas. I know this song by heart and have sung along to it numerous times over the years.

However, when listening to the lyrics this time, I heard them in a new way. I related the loss of the partner in this song to the loss of my grandchild. I started to cry. Then I started to sob. I should have pulled my car over to the side of the road, but I did not. If I had to do it over again, I certainly would have pulled over. But I turned to another radio station instead and kept driving while crying. For me, the words of this song hit too close to home. That Monday morning gave me no warning of what was to be...

Monday, Monday, so good to me
Monday mornin', it was all I hoped it would be
Oh Monday mornin', Monday mornin' couldn't
guarantee
That Monday evenin' you would still be here with me

Monday, Monday, can't trust that day
Monday, Monday, sometimes it just turns out that way
Oh Monday mornin' you gave me no warnin' of
what was to be
Oh Monday, Monday, how could you leave and
not take me

Every other day, every other day
Every other day of the week is fine, yeah
But whenever Monday comes, but whenever
Monday comes
A-you can find me cryin' all of the time
("Monday Monday" from the album *If You Can Believe
Your Eyes and Ears* by The Mamas & the Papas, 1966)

Yes, for a long while you could find me crying on a Monday. But I kept my feelings to myself. I told no one about my feelings of sorrow over the loss of my first grandchild. No one, not even my husband, and especially not my daughter, knew how I was feeling because I kept silent about my true feelings. I kept my grief a secret. Now when this song comes on the radio, I can listen to it and even sing along again. Oftentimes even without crying. It took quite some time to come out of this dark hole... an emptiness, a void, a hollowness that you would not wish upon anyone. But slowly, I did. I found the courage to speak

27

up about my secret sorrow to my sister and a dear friend I have known since childhood. I describe how I accomplished this feat later in this book.

Before I fine-tuned communication techniques to talk about my secret sorrow, I continued to hear stories from family members, friends, co-workers, and neighbors about their grandchildren. I also heard many, many stories about anticipated grandchildren. These grandchildren began to arrive, and I would learn of their birth stories. Some were now first-time grandparents as I expected to be. Some of them were having a subsequent grandchild. I was relieved that these pregnancies were uneventful, or if the pregnancy was eventful, there was a healthy mother and baby in the end. Yet, I still felt an emptiness in my life.

To be completely honest, I must admit that at times I was envious when I heard from a friend or family member that their son or daughter was expecting a baby. Even so, I kept my feelings to myself. I believed that only a selfish person would have feelings of envy over such happy news as an expectant baby. I sometimes had periods of jealousy when these babies arrived, and I saw photos of these new happy families. This was not the real me. No, this was not the real me at all! Privately, I felt guilt and embarrassment about my feelings. However, I told no one.

Maybe you have had a similar experience. These emotions were not what I was accustomed to experiencing throughout my life. I am not typically a jealous person. I hated feeling this way when such feelings surfaced. I had to tell myself that this is not who I am as a person. To move on from these feelings, I reflected that in my life I have so much going on that brings me fulfillment and joy. I have a husband and children I love, who also love me in return. I have a job that makes me feel like I am contributing in a positive way to healthcare. I have good health overall. These are my facts. But not having a grandchild by this point in my life was also a fact. It was my truth.

So, I kept coming back to questions that needed to be answered for my peace of mind. Now that these family members, friends, co-workers, and neighbors are now grandparents, what am I? Someone who was "almost" a grandparent? Someone who longs to be a grandparent, but due to fate is still waiting? Someone who will never be a grandparent? The last option really, really, frightens me.

I pondered these questions over time and thought I would find a book or shorter pamphlet written by someone who had a similar experience as myself. I went to my local bookstore and searched the Loss and Grief section. This section of the bookstore had many resources pertaining to loss and grief. The publications ranged from divorce to the loss of a pet and other grief related topics in between, yet there was no resource about my specific circumstance. I did an internet search and had no luck there either. The closest literature I found were a few books that focused on grandparents who lost a grandchild after birth from various reasons. I was relieved for these grandparents that there are some publications that may be helpful to them during their grieving. I must admit that I was frustrated that I could not find anything in print written for men or women who are grieving because they long to be a grandparent but are not one. I was incredibly disappointed by my dead end. Truthfully, I thought my dead end was more like a sinkhole.

I thought that I could not possibly be the only person in the world who had this experience and felt these emotions. My feelings were validated by my friend Karen. We were coworkers for over ten years. Even so, I never knew her journey as a parent and as a non-grandparent. This goes to show you how much people keep painful feelings to themselves. When she courageously told me her story, I knew that my longing to be a grandparent was not something that was only happening to me. Karen revealed:

"I was 38 when I decided to have a child as a single parent. I did not want to live my life without children. After months of infertility and grief, I had a beautiful son. In spite of a difficult pregnancy and an emergency delivery, the minute I held him I wanted a second. Unfortunately, I could not have a second one but as a special blessing, I have an adopted son. Although this is not about grandparenting, it sets the stage I believe for the feeling of grief about not having grandchildren. I thought that this was perfect, and it is. But the same longing for grandchildren has creeped in as I began to notice that all my friends and my sister had grandchildren. I had thought I would never have children and am happy with my blessings but still feel the grief. Although, I know it is a possibility, neither of my adult children are married and due to special circumstances, may not have children. Although my oldest is seeing someone and thinking about marriage, she may not be able to have children. My second son has difficulty in relationships so I am not certain that he will marry or have children. There is always a chance but meanwhile I often feel the sadness when I am around others who have grandchildren or my sister's grandchildren. I am happy for them and love being with the children, but there is the longing."

I could really identify with Karen's story! As I revealed earlier in this chapter, I too had an infertility history. My daughter's miscarriage brought some of my emotions from my own pregnancy losses back to the surface. This was compounded by my yearning to be a grandparent. My longing to be a grandparent resurfaced each time I heard that someone was going to be a grandparent, someone posted about their grandchild on social media, or someone personally showed me photos of their grandchild. I came back to the reality that a few years ago I too was going to be a grandparent. Then my sadness would reemerge.

I wished there was something I could read, even an article if not a book, to help me process my feelings of loss. I wanted to know that I was not alone in my feelings. I wanted to learn some strategies that helped others on this rough cobblestone path of healing. I began thinking that maybe I should be the person who writes something about this topic. I would think about this, then get distracted by day-to-day life, work, and family responsibilities. Time went on and my distractions got in the way… again and again.

Surprisingly, I experienced a "tipping point" that gave me the push I needed!

My tipping point occurred on Christmas Eve 2016. My husband and I attended an early Christmas Eve church service because we were scheduled to travel out of town on Christmas morning. The 8PM Christmas Eve church service would have gotten us home at 9:30PM and most likely meant going to bed after 11PM… way too late for us to turn around and drive 100 miles early on Christmas morning! So, we opted for the 4PM Family Liturgy at our church. The Family Liturgy is mainly attended by families with young children. This service includes a children's choir, orchestra with children playing drums and chimes, and a play where children act out roles associated with the Nativity. I had attended this service many times in the past and enjoyed its focus on families. This time, the experience proved to be quite different for me.

Even though we arrived 15 minutes prior to the start of the services, the church was already almost filled to capacity. I walked up a side aisle to the middle of the church and saw a pew that had a small amount of room left in it. My husband and I squeezed into this pew. I entered first and he sat to my right, on the aisle. On my left side was a woman who looked my age, but whom I had never seen at church before.

After just a few minutes, the children who were participating in the nativity play started to take their places on, and around, the altar. When this happened, the woman sitting next to me turned my way and whispered to me that she had three grandchildren in today's nativity performance. She pointed out who they were among the children gathered around the altar... two little girls and a little boy, who looked to be two to seven years old. She told me that the two girls had been participating in the nativity play for the last three years. She said she had not missed a Christmas Eve service at church during this time. She was smiling and her face beamed as she spoke.

This woman had every right to be proud! I smiled at her and said something like, "Oh that's wonderful." She then took me by surprise when she asked me, "Who are you here to see? Are your grandchildren in the choir or the Nativity?" Truthfully, I was shocked by her personal questions! Oh boy! I was not expecting this! I kept my smile

(I think I did) and told her, "No one I know is in the choir or the play… I'm here for the services."

I then began to feel uncomfortable. I thought about the grandchild I lost a couple years ago. I realized that he or she would almost be old enough now to be one of the toddlers up on the altar during this service. Then the sadness hit me. I became overwhelmed by resurfaced feelings about the loss of my grandchild. I had not felt like this for quite some time. I entered the church to attend Christmas Eve services never expecting to have memories of the loss of my grandchild come back to the surface, especially not so instantly and deeply. The memories were coming back to me in a public place, not where I had any privacy at all. What if I started to cry?

What if this woman continues to make comments to me about her grandchildren? I felt my face flushing and my mouth getting dry. I felt my heart start to race also. I felt like I was beginning to have a panic attack. I really wanted to change seats. I looked around the church but by now there were no seats left. People were standing in the rear of the church, too. I quickly realized I had to remain where I was seated. So, I picked up a hymnal that was in the pew and started looking through it to avoid any further conversation. While I was looking through the hymnal, I took some slow deep breaths. I reminded myself that the services were going to start soon and everything was going to be ok.

Nonetheless, now I was truly distracted from the Christmas Eve Mass. It felt like just a short time ago I was making plans for my future as a grandparent. The unexpected "happened while I was making other plans." I had to concentrate really hard on the church services that I was here for on Christmas Eve. I was not here to see a child acting, singing, or playing. I began to think about the children participating in this service. Would I ever attend a Christmas Eve service where *my* grandchild had a role in the nativity, was singing in the children's choir, or was playing a musical instrument?

Then my mind started to wander further. I began thinking about other events that children routinely participate in. I thought about plays, recitals, musical and sporting events that take place in schools and in the community. Would I ever be attending one of those events to see my grandchild participate? I really had to force myself to focus on the Christmas Eve services. I had to bring myself back to what was happening during the church services many, many times that evening. And then, unexpectedly, I had a revelation.

That stranger's questions were truly a Christmas gift to me! Our encounter was the push I needed to write this book. Towards the end of the Christmas Eve services, I told myself: "You need to write about 'almost' being a grandparent, the grief you experienced with the loss of

Phoenix, how you kept your sorrow to yourself, and how you learned to speak about your feelings to cope day to day. This could possibly help others who are going through a similar experience." Even while still in church, I kept coming back to an important question: If I am not a grandparent, then who am I?

On the day after Christmas, while I was at home alone folding laundry and still pondering my question, a thought came to me out of the blue! I recalled learning in English classes in school that the prefix "non" meant "not" or "the absence of." Adding "non" to a word changed the word completely. Think about it... non-refundable, non-smoker, non-believer. To be sure I was not mistaken, I immediately went to my computer and looked up the prefix "non" via an online dictionary source. Merriam Webster (2016, 2024) defines non in a few ways. The first definition states the prefix *non* means "not, reverse of, other than" and uses the term non-toxic as an example. Another definition of *non* from this dictionary is "lacking the usual especially positive characteristics of the thing specified" and uses the term non-celebration as an example. These definitions validated my perception.

I now had a name to describe myself in relation to being a grandparent. **I am a non-grandparent.**

Reflections

Write in your responses immediately,
or ponder the questions and return later to write.

What encounters have you experienced with people questioning you about your grandparent status such as I described in the Christmas Eve story?

How did you respond at the time of these encounters?

Are you satisfied with your responses? If so, why? If not, what might you say or do differently if it happened again?

List three things you hope to learn by reading this book.

If any other thoughts come up, feel free to write them here. Your concerns may be addressed later in the book.

CHAPTER 2

The Big G:
Stats and Facts

"A grandparent will help you with your buttons, your zippers, and your shoelaces, and not be in any hurry for you to grow up." Erma Bombeck

I feel like I am surrounded by many, many grandparents in my daily life. Maybe you feel this way too. Living as a non-grandparent in a grandparenting world is hard for me to do at times. Maybe it is hard for you too. I felt like I did not know enough about grandparents, even though I long to be one. So, I searched for information about grandparents from reputable publications that focused on grandparents and grandparenting.

There are as many definitions of the term "grandparent" as there are dictionaries. I used two trustworthy dictionary sources, The Cambridge English Dictionary and Merriam Webster Dictionary, for the definitions in this chapter. The first known use of the term "grandparent" is documented in 1574 (Merriam Webster, 2021). After this time, more began to be written about "grandparent" and other words that families use to describe the male or female in this role. Merriam Webster (2024) defines a *grandparent* as "a parent of one's father or mother." The Cambridge English Dictionary (2024) defines a *grandparent* as "the father or mother of a person's father or mother."

I noticed that both dictionaries' definition of the term "grandparent" implies someone who is *biologically* related to another person. The dictionary definition of the term "grandparent" does not include any emotional attachment or desire to engage in activities with the biological relative. This is not my perception of a grandparent. Maybe it is not your perception either.

My perception of a grandparent goes beyond a strict biological definition. I believe that grandparents are persons who are *actively engaged* with their grandchildren. These can be biologically related persons and can also be non-biological people, such as someone who has an adopted grandchild, a foster grandchild, or someone married to a person whose child has a child. My thoughts about grandparenting are based on my personal experiences in life with my own grandfather, my parents, and my in-laws' interactions with our daughters as well as observations of other grandparents I know, or I see in public. This includes interactions that are both physical (such as playing games together) and emotional (such as laughing with each other) between grandparent and grandchild.

I wondered just how many grandparents there are in the United States (U.S.)? I also thought: what roles do grandparents play in the lives of their grandchildren? To answer these questions, I looked for reputable sources to get a perspective of the number of grandparents in the U.S. and the contributions that grandparents give to their families and to society as a whole.

When I searched for this information about grandparents, I found some interesting facts and statistics about grandparents. What I found reinforced my belief about grandparents being people who are not merely biologically related to their grandchild/grandchildren. I found that grandparents are people actively engaged with a grandchild/grandchildren in many ways. Some facts were both enlightening and stunning for me to learn. Statistics about the average age of a grandparent in the U.S. was the most surprising new information for me. Allow me to share some of the information I found.

One organization that publishes information for the public aged 50+ is the American Association of Retired Persons (AARP). Dr. Ethel Percy Andrus, a retired high school principal, founded AARP in 1958 (AARP, n.d.).

AARP has conducted two major surveys on grandparents and grandparenting. One survey was conducted in 2011 and the most current survey was conducted in 2018. Some of the major results of these surveys are similar; some results from 2018 shed new light on grandparents in the contemporary U.S.

In 2012, results of the survey conducted in 2011 by AARP "Insights and Spending Habits of Modern Grandparents" was published. The author who compiled this report is Cheryl Lampkin, PhD. This report provides a snapshot of the experiences, triumphs, and challenges of grandparents age 50+ (Lampkin, 2012, p.1). The report findings included the results of two grandparenting studies conducted in 2011. One study involved in-depth personal interviews with grandparents age 50 and older. The second study was a national telephone survey of grandparents 50+.*

* The telephone survey method used telephone interviews with a sample of 1,904 U.S. grandparents aged 50 and older selected at random. The interviews were conducted in English and Spanish by Woelfel Research, Inc. from August 25 to October 6, 2011. (Lampkin, 2012, p.3). Respondents in the random sample were ages 50 and over with nearly one-fifth (19%) between ages 50-59, about a third (32%) between ages 60 and 69, and nearly half (46%) ages 70 or older. The majority (69%) were women and three in ten (31%) were men (Lampkin, 2012, p.13).

Some facts reported by Lampkin (2012) did not explicitly state whether they were obtained from the in-depth personal interviews or the telephone survey. However, these facts show that grandparents not only do many activities with their grandchild/grandchildren but they also impart values and beliefs to them as they grow up. "Grandparents do a lot of things with their grandchildren. Grandmothers were more likely than grandfathers to say they go shopping (65% v 58%) or cook or bake (63% v 48%) with their grandchildren. Grandfathers were more likely to say they do physical activities like exercise or play sports with their grandchildren (63% v 56%). Grandparents see their role as shapers of another generation. Specifically, grandparents mentioned the importance of passing on values and helping their grandchildren develop morally and spiritually" (Lampkin, 2012, p. 1).

In 2019, results of an AARP survey conducted in 2018 "Grandparents Today National Survey: Population Report" was published, compiled by authors Patty David and Brittne Kakulla, PhD. This report builds upon the previous AARP survey conducted in 2011. These authors cite that the main objective of the survey was to explore modern grandparent topics/trends/issues to help fully understand the evolving role of grandparents today. Similarly to the grandparent survey conducted in 2011, this report included the results of two grandparenting studies conducted in 2018. One study involved in-depth personal interviews with grandparents age 48+. The second study was a national telephone survey of grandparents between 43 and 76 years old who saw their grandchild(ren) at least twice a year.*

*The online survey targeted grandparents aged 38 and older and took approximately 20 minutes to complete. The number of grandparents completing this survey was 2,654. The telephone survey method used telephone interviews with a sample of ten U.S. grandparents aged between 43 and 76 who saw their grandchild (ren) at least twice a year. The interviews were conducted in English, Spanish and Mandarin by Hotspex Inc. on July 26 and 27, 2018 (David, P. & Kakulla, B., 2019).

Highlights from the *2018 AARP Grandparents Today National Survey* include the following major points:

▷ The youngest grandparents are 38 years of age, with the average age having a first grandchild being 50; this is an increase of two years since 2011 where the average age was 48 years of age;

▷ Most grandparents have, on average, four to five grandchildren; this is a decrease from 2011 where those surveyed reported having on average seven grandchildren;

▷ A strong majority (73%) of the grandparents surveyed enjoy their role and rate their performance as high, up from 66% in 2011;

▷ Grandparents spend a total of $179 billion per year on their grandchildren, approximately $2,562 per grandparent. These dollars go towards a variety of things, from day-to-day costs to gifts to education;

▷ While grandparents make valuable financial contributions to their grandchildren, they also share wisdom and guidance, thereby providing a moral compass;

▷ Grandparents also contribute to their grandchildren's well-being by babysitting; one in ten live in the same household as their grandchildren and 5% of these are primary caregivers to their grandchildren;

▷ A third of those surveyed have grandchildren of a different race or ethnicity; nearly all grandparents say it's important that their different race/ethnicity grandchild knows about the heritage they share; seven in ten make an effort to help their grandchildren learn about the heritage they do not share;

▷ Distance and busy schedules are challenging but grandparents find ways to connect with grandchildren; over half of the participants have at least one grandchild who lives more than 200 miles away and about one-third live approximately 50 miles from their closest grandchild;

▷ Grandparents increasingly adopt new technologies, such as group texting and video chats; as grandparents' use of new technology increases, the use of phone calls to contact grandchildren decreases. Only 46% said they communicated with their grandchildren by phone in 2018, down from 70% in 2011;

▷ Grandparents report that having grandchildren has a positive impact on mental health (68%);

▷ Grandchildren help make grandparents more sociable (67%) and more physically active (65%);

▷ Grandparents nurture grandchildren in-person by:

> Going out to eat 72%

> Having a family celebration 62%

> Watching TV or videos at home 55%

> Going shopping 46%

> Going on outings (e.g., movies, museums, sporting event, etc.) 44%

> Taking trips / travel / vacation 40%

> Attending a school event in which their grandchild was participating 37%

> Cooking or baking together 35%

> Doing physical activities together 32%

All these highlights from the 2018 AARP survey were enlightening for me to read. But they also took my breath away! I thought I would be doing many of these same things with a grandchild by this time in my life. Mostly, I found the last bulleted item above, "how grandparents nurture grandchildren in-person" to be the one specific topic area that had the most profound effect on me in terms of my longing to be a grandparent. These nine statements that grandparents report helps them nurture a grandchild/children are the exact activities that I thought I would be doing with a grandchild by this time of my life. Not doing these activities contributes to some of my sorrow as a non-grandparent. Maybe you also feel a void if you are not doing these types of activities with a grandchild by this time in your life.

The findings from these surveys made me realize that at my age, in my 60s, my desire to be a grandparent was not some fantasy. The real world consists of grandparents both younger and older than me. The real world also consists of persons with an average number of four to five grandchildren. The response from persons who took the 2011 AARP survey that they had an average number of seven grandchildren was stunning to me. Are you surprised to learn this too?

Because I feel that I am constantly surrounded by grandparents in my daily life, I wanted to know how many grandparents there are in the U.S. I looked for the numbers and it didn't take me long to find an answer.

The 2018 AARP Grandparent Survey reported that since 2001, the number of grandparents in the U.S. has grown by 24%, from 56 million to 70 million (David, P. & Kakulla, B., 2019). I think that 70 million grandparents just in the U.S. alone is a colossal number of people!

Another source I found that contained relevant information about grandparents and grandparenting came from The Metropolitan Life Insurance Company (MetLife). MetLife has a center of expertise in aging, longevity, and the generations called the MetLife Mature Market Institute. The Institute, along with the national organization Generations United, published "Grandparents Investing in Grandchildren: The MetLife study on how grandparents share their time, values, and money." (MetLife Mature Market Institute and Generations United, 2012, Cover Page).*

*The study was done via an online survey conducted by Harris Interactive on behalf of the MetLife Mature Market Institute between April 4, 2012 and April 11, 2012. The nationally representative sample included 1,008 grandparents age 45 or older who were selected from among Harris Interactive's online research panel (MetLife, p. 37).

This study examined grandparents' preferences and goals, their connections with their grandchildren, and the levels of care they provide – from long distance grandparents to those who provide regular babysitting and care to the growing number living in multi-generational households or personally raising grandchildren. (MetLife, p. 2). The average number of grandchildren of the participants in the study was four (MetLife, p. 7).

The Executive Summary of this survey reports that among all grandparents participating in the survey, 13% provide care for grandchildren on a regular basis.

Grandmothers reported that they care for grandchildren more frequently than grandfathers; 15% of all grandmothers in the survey provide care on a regular basis as compared to 9% of grandfathers. Younger grandparents of both genders under the age of 65 are more likely to provide care. The majority (74%) of grandparents caring for grandchildren on a regular basis are caregiving/babysitting. Approximately 33% are caregiving five or more days per week; 42% are caregiving fewer than five days a week; 10% are regularly providing other types of care (MetLife, pp. 11-12).

The responses found in the MetLife survey contains a great deal of information about how grandparents share their time with their grandchild/grandchildren. The results of this survey confirmed my belief that grandparents spend a great deal of time interacting in some way with their grandchild/grandchildren. This interaction includes caregiving/babysitting on a regular basis. This is an area of grandparenting that I also believed I would be doing with a grandchild. Not having a grandchild to babysit or care for contributes to some of my sorrow as a non-grandparent.

Back in 2016, the editors of Grandparents.com conducted an internal survey to their members and published *Surprising Facts About Grandparents: We reveal how today's grandparents are defying stereotypes*. This publication includes 16 "facts" about grandparents in contemporary society. I found that four "facts" in this article about grandparents particularly stood out to me. These facts are that grandparents:

1. Represent one-third of the population with 1.7 million new grandparents added to the ranks every year.
2. Are younger than ever before: 3% became grandparents in their 50s, 37% in their 40s, with the average age of becoming a grandparent in this country is 48.
3. Love being grandparents.
4. Like to spend time with their grandkids.

Additionally, overall the Grandparents.com survey results found that of grandparents:

▷ 72% think being a grandparent is the single most important and satisfying thing in their life.
▷ 63% say they can do a better job caring for grandchildren than they did with their own children.
▷ 68% think being a grandparent brings them closer to their adult children.
▷ 90% enjoy talking about their grandkids to just about everyone.

I read these statistics over and over again many times. To me, they confirm how vital the active role of grandparenting is and validate my sorrow being a non-grandparent.

As a non-grandparent, I can only imagine the satisfaction I will get from being actively engaged in the grandparent role. I have already accomplished several goals in my personal life and professional nursing career that have given me great satisfaction. Along with my husband, I raised our daughters to be humble, yet self-confident women. Professionally, I have had great fulfillment from my work with families, community members and nursing students. I am ready to move into a new, unchartered territory in my life as a grandparent. I believe that being a grandparent would be extremely satisfying to me at this time in my life. I yearn to be actively involved with a grandchild. I dream of doing some of the same things that my parents did with our children while they were growing up. My former colleague's husband, Tim, told me his story:

> "I think I would enjoy being a grandfather because I had some very good role models, especially my maternal grandfather and my father. My grandfather was a very caring, fair, tolerant, but firm man who I have many fond memories of that have shaped me. I got to see my father as a grandfather which was a gift! Unfortunately, not long enough time, which my wife and I both regret. I remember vividly at one birthday of our oldest son, he made an old-school scooter from a wooden milk crate, a board, and old roller skates for our younger son so that he did not feel left out. My father (at age 64) then proceeded to demonstrate riding it down the hilly street in front of our house! I think I would greatly enjoy a similar experience with a grandchild."

I can really identify with Tim's story. Maybe you can too.

As with most parents, my parenting style evolved with trial and error. I watched videos, read published material, and listened to family and friends describe how they handle aspects of child rearing. But until an event happened to me in real time, such as my child throwing a temper tantrum in the middle of the mall, my responses were all hypothetical. I believe that due to my maturity and life experiences, I will do a better job caring for my grandchildren than I did caring for my own children.

I was always close with my daughters as they were growing up. However, my husband and I set firm boundaries. We were their parents, not their friends. We knew they were aware of this by things they said when they were frustrated with us. We were often told: "Everyone else is allowed to go to the mall on a school night!" We raised them to know they could come to us with any problem without judgment. I remain close to them now that they are adults. Today, they both live independently but 100 miles from my home. However, we remain in close contact. We routinely talk on the phone or text message, oftentimes daily. We have lunch together at least monthly just to catch up. They spend overnight time seasonally at my home as I live in a community with lake and pool amenities. We spend major holidays together. We celebrate our birthdays together...

not necessarily on the actual date but sometime during the "birthweek." I am not certain that a grandchild would bring me any closer to them, but it might due to a shared experience of parenthood.

Like all the grandparents I know, I envision that I will talk a lot about my grandchildren. I think I will most likely talk about their developmental milestones and their accomplishments. Talking about a grandchild with another grandparent may flow naturally. However, if I know that someone is a non-grandparent, I will talk much less about my grandchildren to them. I may say nothing at all about my potential grandchild if I am aware that they are having a difficult time right now. Due to my experiences as a non-grandparent, I will be sensitive to those I am speaking to about my grandchild/grandchildren, when, and if, this time comes.

The Grandparents.com editors also delved deeper into "spending time with grandchildren" and found these facts:

- ▷ 60% live close to their grandchildren.
- ▷ 46% wish they could live even closer.
- ▷ 70% see the kids at least once a week.
- ▷ 66% travel with their grandkids.
- ▷ 81% have their grandkids for part, or all of, their summer vacation.
- ▷ 55% play videogames with their grandchild.

I re-read these facts several times. They confirm the social and emotional component of being a grandparent that moves well beyond the strict biological textbook definition.

Depending on traffic, I now live 90-120 minutes from my daughters. When I am fortunate to have a grandchild, I believe I will wish that I lived closer to them.

The majority of grandparents surveyed see their grandchildren weekly. I also believe that I would want to see a grandchild at least weekly. When my children were younger we lived about a 20-30 minute drive (in opposite directions) from each set of grandparents. I visited my parents with my daughters weekly. My parents visited us weekly also. Visits to my husband's parents were every two weeks and they visited us at least monthly. Our daughters grew up knowing their grandparents and anticipating family visits. To this day they still reminisce about some of the memories they have visiting the home of each set of grandparents. They remember playing in my parent's backyard, swinging on the solo swing left on an old swing set, and watering flowers in my father's garden. They remember the steep indoor steps at my in-laws' home and how much fun they had coming down them on their behinds bumping downward all the way. They also remember their kitchen table which was a booth configuration. They always felt like they were somewhere special when they sat in the booth! I hope that my future grandchild will have many memories of time spent with me.

I have witnessed family members and friends with a grandchild/grandchildren spending time together on the beach and seen photos of vacations with grandchildren in Disney World. I long to do similar things with a future grandchild. I currently live in a community with a lake. In the summer months my husband and I see many families using the lake facilities for swimming, volleyball, kayaking, and cooking meals. In the future, spending time at our community lake, traveling, and vacationing are also things I dream of doing with a grandchild/grandchildren. I want to help a grandchild with their "buttons, zippers, and shoelaces." You may have these same dreams too.

Reading these survey reports and articles reinforced my belief that when I have a grandchild my life would be enriched in a way I can only imagine now. Reading these reports and articles also validated my sorrow as a non-grandparent. Maybe you also can identify with similar feelings, no matter what circumstance has led you to be a non-grandparent. You are not alone.

Reflections

What statistics about grandparents were surprising for you to learn about? Why?

After reading some facts about grandparents, what facts were new to you?

What facts about how grandparents spend time with their grandchildren were you surprised to read about? Why?

After reading some of the survey results about grandparenting roles, which roles lead to some sorrow for you because you are not doing them at this time in your life?

Place other thoughts here:

CHAPTER 3

The Big N:
Who is a Non-Grandparent?

"Knowing yourself is the beginning of all wisdom."
Aristotle

In Chapter 2, the term grandparent was defined according to definitions found in trustworthy dictionaries. These definitions focus on what has traditionally been associated with the title of "grandparent." Unfortunately, this focus is strictly on a biological relationship between a child and their parent's parent.

This chapter expands upon the conventional dictionary description of the term grandparent to include my interpretation of what "grandparent" and "grandparenting" truly mean. I do this because research findings demonstrate that the role/roles of a grandparent are active ones and vital to both families and society. I go on to introduce my interpretation of the terms non-grandparent and non-grandparenting to provide clarity to these titles. This gives you a viewpoint on what these family relationships entail on an emotional and an attachment level, not merely a biological level.

The biological focused definition of a grandparent that is found in a dictionary is clearly incomplete and therefore inaccurate. Long ago I read a quote by Wade Boggs: "Anyone can be a father, but it takes someone really special to be a dad." I could paraphrase Mr. Boggs statement to be relevant to grandparenthood: "Anyone can have a grandchild but it takes someone really special to be an engaged grandparent." (Mary Ellen Miller).

In my perspective, the emotional attachment and desire to actively engage with a grandchild is what constitutes being a grandparent. A non-grandparent is not merely someone whose child doesn't have a child. The key feature that makes someone truly a non-grandparent is their *great desire or longing* to be a grandparent and actively engage in roles associated with grandparenting, but for various life circumstances this is not occurring. Being a non-grandparent entails the absence of taking on grandparenting roles, such as the numerous activities discussed in the previous chapter.

Non-grandparenting involves "not doing grandparenting things" and not being in the role of a grandparent. This is my biggest difficulty as a non-grandparent. The desire to engage in the grandparenting role can range from small activities (coloring together or taking a grandchild to the park or the movies) to more grand activities (taking family vacations together to Disney World) and every activity you can think of in between. Some of the grandparenting roles I desire to participate in are babysitting, having sleepovers, going on family vacations, and lots and lots of day-to-day activities. Some of these may be grandparenting roles you desire to participate in too.

In addition to activities, I believe I would impart some of my values and beliefs to a grandchild also. When I first heard the song "Humble and Kind," recorded by country music artist Tim McGraw, the lyrics recalled the life lessons my husband and I taught to our daughters:

> Hold the door, say please, say thank you,
> don't steal and don't cheat and don't lie,
> I know you got mountains to climb
> but always stay humble and kind.
> When the dreams you're dreaming come to you,
> when the work you put in is realized,
> let yourself feel the pride
> but always stay humble and kind.
> ("Humble and Kind" from the album *Damn Country Music* by Tim McGraw, lyrics by Lori McKenna, 2016)

My husband and I raised our daughters to be humble and kind, to respect others, and to value people as individuals. These life lessons transcend time and are as relevant now as they were over 30 years ago while raising our daughters. These are some of the same values that I foresee imparting to my future grandchildren also.

So far, I have discussed my being a non-grandparent due to my specific life circumstances. My daughter has a history of infertility and once she became pregnant (with infertility treatment) she had a life shattering pregnancy loss. However, not having a grandchild can occur from many causes. Some types of non-grandparents can be from reasons due to childbearing; some types are caused by reasons other than childbearing. I discuss the many reasons one can be a non-grandparent in this chapter. I am keenly aware of the childbearing types of non-grandparents based upon my personal experience and my professional experience as a maternal-child nurse. As I wrote this book, I became aware of several other types of non-grandparents.

After an article I wrote about non-grandparent grief was published, I learned that I deeply hurt parents who lost an only child and would never have a grandchild. I described how these parents enlightened my perspective on non-grandparents in the Introduction section of this book. By talking to friends who were in blended marriages, I learned about the challenges they face oftentimes not being fully accepted as a grandparent. My focus on childbearing types of non-grandparents was extremely narrow. Gratefully, my view was tremendously expanded.

I also became aware of a particular type of non-grandparent when I watched a YouTube video where Mr. Alex Trebek, of the TV gameshow *Jeopardy* fame, was interviewed by Canadian reporter Lisa LaFlamme. This type of non-grandparent is someone who has a grave medical diagnosis. During this interview titled "Alex Trebek on his health, family, and legacy," Mr. Trebek spoke about his family. He stated, "It does bother me that I may pass on before having a grandchild." His family was off stage, and to break the ice a bit (I believe) he then turned to them and said "hint, hint" to his children (LaFlamme, n.d.).

Mr. Trebek then went on to place this same sentiment on page 283 in his book *The Answer Is... Reflections on My Life* (2020), when he wrote:

> "I'm about to turn eighty. I've lived a good, full life, and I am nearing the end of it. I know that. The only thing that might bother me is if I pass on before I have grandchildren (hint, hint)."

Mr. Trebek passed before having a grandchild. Now I am enlightened about the sorrow that may be present for non-grandparents who face an uncertain future due to their health.

A listing and discussion of the specific types of non-grandparents is found below. You may identify with one or more of the categories listed. As I admitted in the Preface of this book, when I address types of non-grandparents,

I may have omitted your particular reason for being a non-grandparent. I do not want to exclude anyone. If this happened, I hope you feel comfortable to contact me so we can discuss your life circumstances. I placed my email contact information in the Epilogue section of this book.

It is vital for me to point out that this listing of types of non-grandparents is not presented in any rank order. Each type of non-grandparent is important to acknowledge.

Childbearing types of a non-grandparent

A non-grandparent is someone who longs to be a grandparent, but has a son or daughter without living children because they have had, or experienced, any of these conditions:

▷ Infertility
▷ An early pregnancy loss/miscarriage(s) in the first trimester of pregnancy
▷ Pregnancy loss in the second or third trimester of pregnancy
▷ A baby who was born still
▷ A baby that died shortly after birth or in the first month of life (neonatal period)
▷ A baby that died due to Sudden Infant Death Syndrome (SIDS)
▷ A grandchild that died at any age, from any cause

According to the Centers for Disease Control and Prevention (CDC) infertility is defined as not being able to get pregnant (conceive) after one year (or longer) of unprotected sex (CDC, 2024a). Because fertility in women is known to decline steadily with age, some health care providers evaluate and treat women aged 35 years or older after six months of unprotected sex. In the U.S., one of five (19%) married women aged 15 to 49 with no prior births are unable to get pregnant after one year of trying. About one of four (26%) women in this group have difficulty getting pregnant or carrying a pregnancy to term (CDC, 2024a). The CDC National Center for Health Statistics (NCHS) reports that in the years 2015-2019, some form of infertility (either subfertility or nonsurgical sterility) was seen in 11.4% of men ages 15 to 49 and 12.8% of men ages 25 to 49 (Nugent & Chandra, 2024). The numbers of men and women who desire to conceive a pregnancy, or who have difficulty carrying a pregnancy to term, are staggering!

Miscarriage (also called early pregnancy loss) is defined as the unexpected loss of a pregnancy prior to the 20th week of gestation. For women who know they're pregnant, about 10 to 20 in 100 pregnancies (10-20%) end in miscarriage. Most miscarriages (80%) happen in the first trimester before the 12th week of pregnancy. Miscarriage in the second trimester (between 13 and 19 weeks) happens in 1-5 of 100 (1-5%) pregnancies. However, these numbers could be higher as some miscarriages occur before a woman knows she is pregnant (March of Dimes, 2024).

Miscarriages can occur for a variety of reasons. The most common factor that may contribute to miscarriage includes a chromosome problem with the fetus. Other possible causes of a miscarriage can be drug and alcohol abuse, hormonal problems, physical problems with the uterus or cervix, or a chronic disease such as diabetes (U.S. National Library of Medicine, 2022). I know from our miscarriage decades ago, and my daughter and son-in-law's pregnancy loss at 11 weeks, how traumatic a life experience this is. No matter what the cause, a miscarriage that occurs when a pregnancy is desired is a life altering loss not only for the pregnant woman and the father of the baby, but for the entire family.

Stillbirths occur when a baby dies in the uterus after the 20th week of pregnancy. Stillbirths are due to natural causes. They can happen before delivery or during delivery. Causes include problems with the placenta and/or the umbilical cord, genetic problems with the fetus, fetal infections, and other physical problems in the fetus. Sadly, in at least half of all cases, it is not possible to tell why the baby died (US. National Library of Medicine, 2021). Stillbirths occur in about 1 in 175 births, and each year about 21,000 babies are stillborn in the U.S. (CDC, 2024b). Usually the pregnancy is uneventful, and the death of the baby happens without any warning. A stillbirth is devastating. A baby born still is a shattering event that affects parents, grandparents, and others who love them. My friend Lilly shared her story about how devastating a stillbirth is for a grandparent and also how she was not supported from women she associated with:

"After many attempts to get pregnant, in their eighth year of marriage my son and daughter-in-law finally announced they were expecting a baby girl. I was over the moon. After all, I was finally fulfilling my "obligation" of becoming a grandparent (it sounds silly when I say that, doesn't it?). Finally, I would be joining the "grandparent" club and be part of the clique. However, that dream was to be shattered when my daughter-in-law went into labor and their beautiful little girl was stillborn. The sorrow is indescribable, and even to this day, almost eight years later, the memory of that phone call from my son, telling me the doctor couldn't find a heartbeat, is like a blow to my chest. At the time, I belonged to a women's organization of 50 women and not ONE of them called me or sent a sympathy card expressing their condolences. This was simply a miscarriage to them, which would have been devastating enough. Years later, when I was discussing the loss of my granddaughter with one of those club women, and how no one acknowledged her death, she told me (and I still cannot believe she said this!), "we didn't think it was a big deal to you." I thank God for my best friend, who was my constant source of comfort and was always there to lend an ear, and her heart, during those devastating days. I don't know what I would have done without her. Even my son's in-laws' thought he and their daughter should 'move on and get over it' after a time. You NEVER recover from that kind of loss. Now, a happy ending: since that time, they have given us two beautiful grandsons. But truth be told, I still mourn for that precious little girl. I suppose I always will."

Lilly's story is one that I believe many readers can relate to. Lack of support to grieving grandparents is common in society. Trite phrases, such as "moving on" and "getting over it" are oftentimes heard by those grieving a loss. I am so sorry if similar experiences may have happened to you too. You deserve so much more!

Childbearing types of non-grandparents also include those who unexpectedly lose an infant grandchild younger than one year of age. This is now called sudden unexpected infant death (SUID) and includes infant deaths from sudden infant death syndrome (SIDS). In 2022, there were about 3,700 sudden unexpected infant deaths (SUID) in the U.S. This includes:

▷ 1,529 deaths from SIDS
▷ 1,131 deaths from unknown causes
▷ 1,040 deaths from accidental suffocation and strangulation in bed (CDC, 2024c)

When an infant dies from SUID, this also is a devastating event for families. The lives of parents, grandparents, and many others are shattered.

A neonatal death happens when a baby dies

in the first 28 days of life. The most common neonatal deaths are in babies who are born premature, have a low birthweight, and/or have birth defects (March of Dimes, 2024). A neonatal death is also a devastatingly shattering event for the entire family. Believe me, I know this trauma. I personally know how devastating a neonatal death is because our first daughter, Marissa, died when she was eight days old due to complications of prematurity. Actually the word "devastating" doesn't even begin to describe my emotions from her loss. I know there are no words that accurately describe the pain associated with the other types of pregnancy loss I have addressed here either.

Additionally, there are no words to describe the pain from the loss of a living grandchild who dies at any age, from any cause. Accidents, cancer, gun violence, the list of causes of death goes on. If this grandchild is your only grandchild, you are now suddenly without grandchildren. During your grieving you may start to wonder "who am I now?"

There are a small number of books in print for grandparents who lose a grandchild. Only six books in print that are not self-published address grandparent grief. Two were published long ago... in the 1990s. The other four books were published from 2005 to 2018. Most focus on those who have lost a living grandchild. One, published in 2005 by Nina Bennett, is written for grandparents who experience stillbirth and infant death. It contains some of the same information as this book, such as grief theories and finding ways to invest energy in daily living. My book builds on this and takes you to a new level. *Secret Sorrow* is intended to help you navigate your new life as a non-grandparent and provide ways to help you communicate your sorrow to others and cope with your loss as you live your day-to-day life.

I am a non-grandparent who falls into the "childbearing" type of non-grandparent. I am a non-grandparent because my daughter has an infertility history. Also, once she conceived her first pregnancy, she had a miscarriage in her 11th week. My status as a non-grandparent is due to two childbearing reasons. You may identify with one or more of these childbearing reasons. No matter the reason you are a non-grandparent, each type is important to recognize. We are not alone in our journey.

Non-childbearing types of non-grandparents

Being a non-grandparent can also be due to reasons that are not related to childbearing issues. I refer to these reasons as non-childbearing types of non-grandparents. I believe there are several non-childbearing types of non-grandparents. A brief description of each follows. Some non-childbearing categories have statistics or estimates of how many people are found in each category. Some do not. Either way, you are not alone in your non-grandparent journey.

Similarly, the non-childbearing reasons are not listed in any order of importance. All non-childbearing types of non-grandparents are important to recognize. All these types may cause grief and profound sorrow for you as a non-grandparent.

You may be a non-grandparent because your son or daughter has decided that they want to delay childbearing. They may be delaying childbearing due to educational or career pursuits. You may be hesitant to ask questions of them about their childbearing choices because you don't want to pry. You may be concerned that asking personal questions about future grandchildren may damage your relationship with your child. You may also feel so very different from friends and family who are having grandchildren. My friend Lilly also shared this story:

> "My son and daughter-in-law got married in 2005 and decided to wait several years before starting a family. I was frequently asked by friends, or even unfamiliar people I encountered, why I didn't have grandchildren. I thought the question quite rude. How could I possibly answer that since I didn't know if it was by my son and daughters-in-law's choice or if they were experiencing difficulty conceiving. During those non-grandparent years, when I yearned to have a grandchild, I would often be in the company

of someone who had a grandchild or grandchildren, who would show me pictures of their little ones. I felt very removed from the conversation, and almost embarrassed for not having my own photos to share. I began to avoid asking people around me about their children, on the off chance they would tell me they've had their first grandchild, or yet another one. Was this their fault? Not at all. Society has programmed us to 'expect' grandchildren by a certain age and if that didn't happen, we were pariahs."

Lilly's life experience may be very similar to yours. I hope you are now aware that you are not alone in your feelings.

You may be a non-grandparent because your child does not plan to have children. Some adults choose to remain childless. Their reasons for their decision are personal ones. It may be very difficult for you to understand and come to terms as to why a child of yours would not want to be a parent themselves. This choice is beyond your control. My colleague and her husband told me their perspectives about being non-grandparents because their adult children are not parents. One child has decided to remain childless. Their oldest child is single and not in a long-term relationship. Joann shared her story with me:

"Our youngest child, now 44 and married for five years, told us before the wedding that they did not plan to have kids. I didn't ask why. I just said to keep an open mind as they might change their plans. My older child (whom I admit I am closer to) told me about ten years ago that he was sorry that he disappointed me by not being married by now with a family. I told him I was disappointed for him, not with him because he is such a good guy. During the early time of Covid-19 he was dating someone for over a year. This dating relationship ended last spring. That was when I knew the dream of my being a grandparent was over."

Her husband's perspective is:

"My wife and I really don't talk about not having a grandchild. I won't bring it up because of the negative feelings it causes her. I am in a different place than she is. We have two children; one is still single, and one is married and told us that they would not be having children. Although being a grandparent is something that I feel I would enjoy, I believe that our children's choice to have children is their own. I would hope that a desire to have children would be something that they would want, not because either we or the world expects it. I tend to be a "control the controllable" kind of guy which helps me not get ahead of myself and prematurely set expectations. However, it is also possible that I am in complete denial and just trying to protect myself from feelings of loss."

I know that oftentimes my husband and I were on different pages discussing our feelings about being non-grandparents. Like Joann's husband, he too likes to be in control of situations. But life throws curveballs, and we can't control everything that happens to us. Currently, more adults are making conscious decisions to be childless.

Childlessness, or the state of being without children (Cambridge English Dictionary, 2024) can be due to childbearing issues as described previously in this chapter, but also due to conscious decisions made by adult men and women to postpone or never have children. According to Schondelmyer "delaying marriage is related to delaying childbirth" (2017, p. 1). In her article, *More Adults Living Without Children*, Ms. Schondelmyer includes the following statistics about U.S. adults:

▷ The median age at first marriage has gone from 20.6 to 27.4 for women and from 23.1 to 29.6 for men since 1967.

▷ The largest change in the proportion of adults living without children happened among those aged 18 to 35; in 1967, the majority of 18-to-24-year-olds had children living with them (53.3%) but by 2016, less than a third did (31.2%).

▷ The changes are even more dramatic among 25-to-34-year-olds; in 1967, 23.9% in that age group did not have their own children under their roof; by 2016, this percentage more than doubled to 61.5%.

A report published by the NCHS sheds light on birthrates in the U.S. This report is based on 2021 provisional U.S. birth data processed by the NCHS as of February 10, 2022. Births by age, race, Hispanic origin of the mother, preterm birth, and cesarean delivery are all included and reveal the first increase in births for several years. The provisional number of births for the U.S. in 2021 was 3,659,289, up 1% since 2020 and the first increase since 2014. The general fertility rate was 56.6 births per 1,000 women aged 15-44. This was up 1% from 2020 and the first increase in the rate since 2014. The total fertility rate was 1,663.5 births per 1,000 women in 2021, up 1% from 2020. Birth rates declined for women in age groups 15-24, rose for women in age groups 25-49, and was unchanged for adolescents aged 10-14 in 2021 (Hamilton et al., 2022).

In the past, delaying parenthood was mainly an option for upper-middle-class Americans. Recently, more women of all social classes have prioritized education and career. Postponing having a child has become a pattern among American women almost everywhere. Professor Caitlin Myers, an economist at Middlebury College who analyzed county-level birth records for The New York Times, conducted a geographic analysis in which the data offers a clue: The birth rate is falling fastest in places with the greatest job growth — where women have more incentive to wait (Tavernise, S., Miller, C., Bui, Q., & Gebeloff, R.,

2021). If your child/children choose childlessness, know that you are not alone.

Additionally, there are other circumstances where an adult child is not having children. You may be a non-grandparent because your son or daughter is transgender without children. Recent reports reveal that 1.6 million people in the U.S. identify as transgender (Williams Institute, n.d.). Your adult child may be exploring their sexual identity, going through a transition or already transitioned to a new sexual identity. Their decision to postpone children or remain childless is an individual, personal choice.

You may be a non-grandparent as a parent of someone who is in a same-sex committed or married relationship. For decades, it was against societal norms for same sex couples to either adopt a child or have a biological child via reproductive technology and/or surrogacy. The pendulum has shifted, and more same sex couples are having children by adoption, reproductive advances, and surrogacy. However, you may have a child in a same sex relationship who has no children. The reason they have no children is a personal one for them. Yet, it may be extremely difficult for you to be without a grandchild from your child.

You may be a non-grandparent because your adult son or daughter is not in a relationship with another adult. Reasons for this vary. Many young adults want to further their educational goals. Oftentimes, young adults put time and energy into their career. These focus areas allow little free time for pursuing a relationship. Or, your adult child may have been in a few relationships, some could even have been long-term, but the relationships did not lead to having a child.

Your child's dating decisions and relationship status are personal ones for them. It may be very painful for you to have adult children without children, because, no matter what the reason is, oftentimes family members and friends who have children of similar ages are all becoming grandparents and you are not. Your feelings are justified. However, your adult childrens' life decisions are theirs to make.

Additional types of non-grandparents:

I think there are also unique situations that create non-grandparents. These circumstances are not listed in order of magnitude. Each one is accompanied by a personal story of loss. There is grieving associated with each personal story.

You may be someone whose only child died before having any children. Your grief is multiplied because you lost your only child *and* any chance for a wished-for grandchild. As I stated in the Introduction, I learned to look beyond the lens of my personal experience and my maternal-child nursing experience by listening to other non-grandparents. The non-grandparents who widened my perspective the most were the women who lost their only child and informed me of how "left out" of society they are when they responded to my online article in *Still Standing Magazine*. I humbly apologized to them. I promised them that I would always include parents who lost their only child in any future writing I do about non-grandparents. I am so deeply sorry for parents who lost an only child for their compound pain and sorrow. I share their stories here to validate the grief experienced by these parents and to expand understanding and recognition.

You may be someone who has an only child with a significant physical or cognitive disability that renders them unable to have a child. I am so deeply sorry for your complex pain and sorrow.

You may be someone who never had children when you were younger, for whatever reason. Now that you are older, some family and friends with children are becoming grandparents. You may be experiencing grief and sorrow because of this. I am so deeply sorry for your pain and sorrow.

You may be someone who now has a serious medical condition and does not have any grandchildren yet. You may have an uncertain future. Or, you may know you are facing the final weeks or months of your life. I am so deeply sorry if you are grieving for this potential lost life experience. I shared Alex Trebek's perspective earlier in this chapter. Countless other non-grandparents face this uncertainty.

I think there are also some extraordinary situations whereby even grandparents can be a non-grandparent. A grandparent may have a grandchild or grandchildren but also have some special circumstances surrounding this grandchild or grandchildren. One of these circumstances is when "estrangement" occurs in the family. You may be a grandparent, however, for whatever reason, you are not permitted by the grandchild's parents to be involved in grandparenting your grandchild(ren). You long to grandparent your grandchild(ren) and you are not permitted to do so. You may feel that you are different from all your family members, friends, and/or co-workers who have grandchildren and are engaged in grandparenting roles. Meg shares her non-grandparent story here:

> Imagine this, me a young girl, giving birth to my first child. He was a sweet little boy. This little boy filled my heart with endless joy. My son grew up and got married. They blessed me with my first grandchild, a joy only a Grand-mom knows. We shared many cherished times together; birthdays, holidays, and vacations. Then imagine this all being ripped away from you like a page being torn out of a book. They decided that they no longer wanted to be part of my life. I often wondered why, and what they told my

grandson. I guess I will never know. The sadness I felt was overwhelming. I finally decided that I could not shed another tear, so I stopped crying. My son and grandson are gone forever.

My heart hurts for Meg. You may be an estranged grandparent also. Or, you may have family or friends who are estranged from their grandchildren. If you do, you may be able to relate to Meg's story.

It is difficult to find the exact number of adult children estranged from a parent or parents. A recent book *Fault Lines: Fractured Families and How to Mend Them*, by Dr. Karl Pillemer a professor at Cornell University, contains staggering statistics. Dr. Pillemer conducted the first large-scale national survey about family estrangement. He found that more than a quarter of the adults in his sample reported being estranged from family members; 10% were estranged from a parent or child (Pillemer, 2020). If you are a non-grandparent due to family estrangement, you are definitely not alone. You need to be supported in your non-grandparent journey.

Additionally, contemporary U.S. families are not all traditional nuclear families. Today, there is great diversity in families. According to the PEW Research Center (2024):

> For 2014, the share of children living in a two-parent household is at the lowest point in more than half a century: 46% are in this type of family arrangement today, compared with 61% in 1980 and 73% in

1960. And even children living with two parents are more likely to be experiencing a variety of family arrangements due to increases in divorce, remarriage, and cohabitation. Some 15% are living with parents in a remarriage and 7% are living with parents who are cohabiting. The declining number of children living in what is often deemed a "traditional" family has been largely replaced by the rising number of children living with single or cohabiting parents.

Another report released by the PEW Research Center in 2018, reveals a growing share of unmarried parents are living with a partner. In 2017, the number of children living with a cohabiting parent had risen dramatically to 35% (Livingston, 2018). This report also addresses how fluid U.S. families have become:

One estimate suggests that by the time they turn nine, more than 20% of U.S. children born to a married couple and over 50% of those born to a cohabiting couple will have experienced the breakup of their parents, for instance. The declining stability of families is linked both to increases in cohabiting relationships, which tend to be less long-lasting than marriages, as well as long-term increases in divorce. Indeed, half of solo parents in 2017 (52%) had been married at one time, and the same is true for about one-third of cohabiting parents (35%).

As these statistics show, the structure of U.S. families is complex. You may be the step-parent of an adult child of your spouse or cohabitating partner. This adult child may have a child or children. Because you are not the biological parent of the adult child of your spouse or partner, you may be considered an "outsider" by them. They may not give you the same opportunities to interact with their child that they give their biological parents, even though their parents are no longer married to each other. This may cause you to experience grief and sorrow. My friend Ruth recently told me her story. I have known her for 50 years, since we attended nursing school together. However, she never told me her story until I told her about my sorrow because I was a non-grandparent. This verifies how oftentimes we tend to keep our feelings to ourselves. I am so grateful to Ruth for opening up to me about her life experience. Her narrative fits into several of the non-grandparent types discussed in this chapter.

> "One of the most significant relationships in my life was with my maternal grandmother who lived in my home as I was growing up. When my mom died at age 56, my grandmother filled that gap. She passed away at age 93. So being a grandparent was a natural yearning in my heart. I have four step-grandchildren now who are grown. When they were younger, I made great effort not to upsurp their bio grandmothers of that role. I have one son in a long-term relationship who I do not believe will have any children. So, I sometimes feel like I am in limbo – I "sort of" have grandchildren, but not really. I am at

peace with this at this point. The thing I will miss the most is the idea of spending time with a grandchild as many of my years growing up were spent in the company of my dear grandmother. But I'm thankful my son is pursuing his life and is happy."

Like Ruth, I believe it is essential that non-grandparents whose child has made a choice to be childless are thankful their child is pursuing their life goals and are happy. Decisions to remain childless are deeply personal ones.

Childbearing, non-childbearing, and all additional types of non-grandparent are important to acknowledge. Being a non-grandparent, no matter what the cause, is a loss of a desired grandchild. This loss can be accompanied by grief, mourning, and the bereavement that is associated with a loss of any kind. The sadness I felt of being a non-grandparent was extremely difficult for me to talk about to other people. I carried my silent grief as a secret sorrow within me for years. One day, I found "the wisdom to know myself." I took a leap of faith and found the courage to speak up. I tell my story about how I finally found the courage to speak up in the next chapter. You deserve to find the courage to speak up too.

Reflections

What non-grandparent type/types apply to you personally? Why?

What grandparenting role/roles do you have some sorrow about
because you are not doing them at this time in your life?

Place other thoughts here:

CHAPTER 4

Secret Sorrow: Finding the Courage to Speak Up

"Nearly everyone has had a box of secret pain, shared with no one." John Steinbeck

It can be hard to talk about feelings of sorrow that come along with being a non-grandparent. I think it relates in great part to our societal norms. I was taught by my parents, and other adults in my life, such as teachers and employers, that when stressful and/or sad times were happening to me that I should "pull yourself up by your bootstraps" and to "keep your chin up." I was also encouraged by these same people to keep personal feelings to myself. "Check your feelings at the door" is a phrase that I have heard numerous times by supervisors in the workforce. In hindsight, these well-meaning people weren't doing me any favors. Maybe you have had experiences like these too.

Based on my life experiences, for a very long time I found it difficult to tell someone other than my immediate family that I am feeling sad about something. It was also hard for me to tell someone other than my close family or close friends that talking about a certain topic is uncomfortable for me. Perhaps you feel this way too. If you do, that is ok. It is important for you to know you are not the only one who has difficulty telling someone you are sad or are having a difficult time with something. Countless others have difficulty talking about their feelings too.

In addition, I am also someone who is sensitive to what others are feeling. My empathy for others is a very good trait to have as a nurse. However, my ability to be empathetic to others' feelings has often resulted in my feelings being placed on the back burner. Now I realize that this is not good for me in the long run.

The main reason I have had difficulty expressing how difficult, and oftentimes sad, it is for me to live as a non-grandparent in a grandparenting world is that I know that other people are going through really difficult times. Many people I know about my age have recently gotten a diagnosis of cancer or some other devastating health news, or they have lost their long term job, or they just found out their child is filing for divorce, or they recently lost their home to foreclosure, etc. I felt that my life situation of being a non-grandparent paled in comparison to what they were experiencing. Hence, I kept my feelings about being a non-grandparent to myself. I did this even when someone was going on and on about their grandchildren and I felt like shouting at them: "Enough about how cute your grandchildren are!" or "Enough about Joey and the new puppy," or "Enough about Julia's dance lessons," or "Can't you talk about anything else at all?!" But I never said any of these things. Maybe you can relate to this too.

However, one day I opened up to my sister Sharon about my desire to be a grandparent and my feelings of sorrow. The way the conversation evolved where I felt the need to confide in her about my secret sorrow was unplanned on my part. We were talking on the phone about various topics. Sharon shared with me that a woman we mutually knew recently told her that she was finally going to be a grandmother after her daughter experienced many years of infertility. Her daughter's pregnancy occurred after several attempts at in-vitro fertilization and was now at 20 weeks gestation. Our mutual friend felt that she could begin to tell people this amazing news.

I remember instantly feeling very relieved for our friend that her daughter's pregnancy was now well into the second trimester. I also was happy for the entire family. But then my contemplation of "would being a grandparent ever happen to me?" began to resurface while still on the phone call with my sister. I can't remember exactly what I said to break the ice on the topic of being a non-grandparent. I do remember asking her if I could confide something to her that I had not confided to anyone besides my husband. I disclosed to her how difficult it was for me to be a non-grandparent at this point in my life. Sharon knew how much I was anticipating the birth of my first grandchild a couple years ago as she was filled with excitement at being a great aunt too. I remember telling her that more and more of the people I knew, family, friends and co-workers, were all now either becoming grandparents or were expecting yet another grandchild. She is a good listener and did not interrupt me. She expressed condolences to me. She said it hadn't dawned on her how difficult it must be for someone to live as a non-grandparent. I thanked her for listening and told her that condolences were not necessary. I told her that having someone to confide in was what I so greatly needed. I felt a great sense of relief as we conversed! I felt like the weight of the world had been lifted from my shoulders. I finally said something about my secret sorrow to someone I loved and trusted!

Approximately one month later, I spoke about these same feelings about being a non-grandparent to a close childhood friend, Marsha, who is a grandmother. Marsha and I have known each other for 50 years. We have a lot of history together, even though after she married she relocated three hours from our hometown. We kept in touch during the time we raised our children and got together whenever she returned to our hometown to visit her family. This time my speaking up about my sorrow was not telephonic, but rather occurred over lunch. I started the conversation by telling Marsha that I had something to confide in her that I had only told my husband and sister about. I told her immediately that she had never made me feel uncomfortable when she speaks about her granddaughter. I told her several other things: that I think that she speaks about her granddaughter in a manner that, like Goldilocks, I think is "just right;" that I appreciate the fact she doesn't talk on and on about her granddaughter where we then have very little other conversation; and that I was also grateful that she shows me a couple recent photos but not a dozen pictures or more of her grandchild. I think she was wondering "where the heck is this conversation going?" I then confided in her about my sorrow associated with being a non-grandparent. My statements to her in person were much the same as my conversation was on the phone with my sister. Marsha also told me she never realized how difficult it must be for a non-grandparent to live in a grandparenting world.

After I opened up about my feelings I received a great deal of support from both my sister and my childhood friend. They had no idea about my feelings of loss and my grief associated with being a non-grandparent. They gave me permission to grieve and to talk about my feelings. They encouraged me to talk in the moment, and also encouraged me to open up to them again in the future whenever I felt like I needed to talk. Their comments validated my feelings. This had a positive long-lasting effect on me. These experiences confirmed the necessity of writing a book that would benefit other individuals who are non-grandparents too.

I encourage you to talk to those closest to you about your feelings associated with non-grandparenting. The first conversation, even though it was with my sister with whom I have a close relationship, was not easy for me to begin and to engage in. The first conversation you have with someone close to you may not be easy to do either. However, once you open up to one person you know and trust, it will be easier for you to do it again... and again... and again.

Once the conversation is underway, because you are confiding in a close family member or friend, you will be speaking about your feelings to someone you love and trust. They love and trust you in return. Love and trust are very powerful in relationships.

After I let my feelings about non-grandparenting be known to these two people I love and trust, I spoke up to more close relatives and friends about my secret sorrow. I used short statements with an open-ended question to get the conversation going about my feelings associated with being a non-grandparent. Some of the statements I used that have been helpful to me are:

▷ I need to talk to you about something personal I have kept to myself for a long time. I know you're a good listener. When can we talk?

▷ I really want to be a grandparent! And you know this is not happening. I need to confide my true feelings to someone I am close to. Because I feel so close to you, I chose to confide in you. When can we talk about this?

▷ I want tell you something that may surprise you. You might be surprised to hear that because I am not a grandparent it is hard for me to be around grandparents/expectant grandparents sometimes. Because I trust you as a friend, when can I talk to you about this?

▷ I feel sad sometimes that I am not a grandparent yet. I want you to know that you have never made me feel uncomfortable when you talk about your grandchildren. I think you are sensitive to the fact that I long for a grandchild but don't have one yet. Because you are so sensitive towards me, I want to talk to you about how I feel. When can we talk?

Notice, I didn't ask my closest family or friend "can we talk about this" or "can I confide in you?" I avoided questions that are close-ended and would give someone a chance to say "no." I used open-ended techniques instead. What do I mean by an open-ended question?

In my psychiatric nursing classes I learned the difference between open-ended and closed-ended questions. Open-ended questions require the respondent to think more about their response. Asking open-ended questions or making an open-ended statement are excellent strategies to use for an in-depth conversation. This is because they require something other than a "yes" or a "no" response from the person you are speaking with. That is what closed-ended questions do... these types of questions allow a person to give a "yes" or "no" response. Here is an example of a close-ended question: "Do you have time today to talk about something important to me?" This gives the responder a chance to say "no." If "no" is their response, then there would be no opportunity to discuss my feelings associated with being a non-grandparent at this moment. If I use a close-ended question, and the answer is "no" then that ends any conversation.

Avoid using close-ended questions when you want to have an important/meaningful conversation. This takes some practice. In reality, it is easier to ask a close-ended question. These are the types of questions we routinely use. However, these types of questions don't delve into a person's feelings, emotions, or specific details. "Did you have a good day at school?" "Yes." "Do you want pizza for dinner?" "No." "Do you have a headache?" "Yes." The list goes on and on.

Open-ended questions or statements can help start a conversation because they can't be answered with one or two words. An open-ended question or statement usually gets the attention of the responder. Once you have their attention, conversation usually will flow. I used open-ended questions to begin my conversations about my secret sorrow to persons I loved and trusted. Once I got their attention, the rest of the conversation flowed. It wasn't exactly easy, but it flowed.

Learning the technique of asking open-ended questions requires some time and some thought. It took me a while, probably most of a semester of nursing school, to get accustomed to asking questions in an open-ended way. Because responses to an open-ended question are more than a simple "yes" or "no" you can engage in a more in-depth conversation with someone. If the response to an open-ended question you receive is not thorough, then another open-ended follow up question should be asked.

Looking over the close-ended questions I used as examples above, changing them to open-ended questions or statements could be: "What was the best, or, what was not the best, part of your day at school today?" "Tell me a couple choices you want for dinner tonight and why you'd like them." "Your facial expression tells me you have another one of your horrible headaches... what happened today to make you feel this way?"

When speaking up about your feelings associated with being a non-grandparent, I encourage you to phrase your conversations in an open-ended way too. Start the conversation by doing the following:

Let your close family member/friend know you have something you want to confide in them about,

Validate them with a positive statement, such as they are a good listener, or you trust them, and

Finish with an open-ended question such as "when can we talk about this?"

I found that the hardest part about letting someone I was close to know how I feel about being a non-grandparent was just starting the conversation. Once I opened up to a close family member or friend about my "box of secret pain" most often the conversation just started to flow.

On a rare occasion, I had the experience where the conversation about being a non-grandparent did not flow easily. On some occasions, the person I was speaking with appeared to be uncomfortable with the direction of the conversation. This might occur to you. If this happens, tell them what you are perceiving. Ask them to be honest with you. Ask them if they would rather not hear about how you are feeling about being a non-grandparent. Ask them if this information is too hard for them to discuss and if they would rather you continue this conversation at some other time, or not at all. This type of reaction may rarely (if ever) occur, but you should be prepared to address it if it does occur. It has been my experience that the persons I have confided in about my feelings associated with being a non-grandparent have been truly touched by my comments, want to listen to my story, and want to do whatever they can to help me in my journey.

Because you are confiding in someone you love and trust you may get emotional during the conversation. You may even cry. If this happens, this is ok. In fact, your family member or friend may be the one who starts to get emotional or cries because they are learning something so sensitive about your feelings about being a non-grandparent. Remember that they care about you, and because of this they will want to listen and to help you with your feelings. They will undoubtedly give you the support you need now, and in the future.

Being a non-grandparent, from whatever reason, is accompanied by specific challenges. In addition to the challenges associated with speaking up about my sorrow, another big challenge for me as a non-grandparent has been dealing with my feelings of loss and grief. Even though I am a nurse, I had to re-learn grief concepts. I did a good deal of reading about loss and grief to write this book. The next chapter delves into the topics of grief, mourning, and bereavement associated with loss.

You may also have some trouble dealing with your feelings of loss as a non-grandparent. As I stated in The Introduction, if your feelings of loss are overwhelming, seek out a healthcare professional for guidance. I should have done so, rather than allowing myself to suffer in silence for so long.

Reflections

Who do you feel most comfortable talking to about your feelings about any subject? (use initials if that makes you feel more comfortable)

Now, who would you feel most comfortable talking to concerning your feelings about being a Non-grandparent? (use initials if that makes you feel more comfortable)

How will you start your first conversation with this person?

How will you respond if they start to cry during this conversation?

What will you do if you begin to cry during this conversation?

Place other notes or thoughts here:

CHAPTER 5

The Non-Grandparent Journey: Grief, Mourning, and Bereavement

"When all is said and done, grief is the price we pay for love." Dr. Colin Murray Parkes

I believe that to understand our own experiences as non-grandparents, it is really important to include information that addresses the concepts of grief, mourning, and the bereavement processes that follow loss. Many times, these terms are used incorrectly. Non-grandparents should be knowledgeable about what each of these concepts is about.

Grief is a primarily emotional reaction to the loss of a loved one through death (Weiss, 2008). More recently, The American Psychological Association (APA) defined grief as "the anguish experienced after significant loss, usually the death of a beloved person. Grief often includes physiological distress, separation anxiety, confusion, yearning, obsessive dwelling on the past, and apprehension about the future. Intense grief can become life-threatening through disruption of the immune system, self-neglect, and suicidal thoughts. Grief may also take the form of regret for something lost, remorse for something done, or sorrow for a mishap to oneself" (APA, 2024).

People can experience grief from any type of loss, not only from the death of a loved one. "Grief can accompany any event that disrupts or challenges our sense of normalcy or ourselves. This includes the loss of connections that define us. You may grieve the loss of:

▷ A friend, family member, partner or pet.
▷ A marriage, friendship or another form of kinship.
▷ Your home, neighborhood or community.
▷ Your job or career.
▷ Financial stability.
▷ A dream or goal.
▷ Good health.
▷ Your youth.
▷ Fertility. (The Cleveland Clinic, 2023, p.1)

Research findings show that loss occurring with infertility, pregnancy, childbirth, or after giving birth is associated with profound grief for parents. There is very limited research to date on the grief responses of grandparents to the loss of a grandchild, either during pregnancy or after birth.

I know that I experienced grief by the loss of my anticipated grandchild. I was excitedly awaiting being a grandmother and doing "everything" associated with the role of a grandparent. Babysitting, walks in the park, traveling to the beach, and even more activities filled my thoughts with the anticipated arrival of my grandchild. When my daughter and son-in-law's pregnancy ended in a miscarriage, my grandchild and my grandparenting roles were no longer my reality.

In the initial days following the miscarriage I spent my time focused on them and their needs. They told me that they wanted my daily company, so I went to their home for a period of time each day. I tried to help with household routines during this time. I, as well as other family members, prepared and delivered meals. I did some light housekeeping and laundry. I went home when I could tell by their cues that they needed privacy and space. Somedays I could see that my daughter was exhausted and needed to nap. Other days I just knew that they needed to spend some time together, just the two of them.

After several days, when they both returned to work, I began to grieve. As a nurse, I am aware that grief is associated with "grief reactions." I began to experience some grief reactions. According to Worden (2008), normal grief reactions may include:

▷ Emotional responses: anger, sadness, sleep and appetite disturbances
▷ Physical sensations: tightness in the throat or chest, breathlessness, lack of energy
▷ Altered cognition: disbelief, confusion, sense of presence of the deceased
▷ Behaviors: crying, sleep and appetite disturbances, social withdrawal

I was sad after the loss of my anticipated grandchild, Phoenix. In the immediate 24 hours, I was in a state of disbelief. Soon after this, I cried. I cried on and off for several days in a row, eventually the crying periods were shorter and less frequent. What lasted a bit longer were my appetite and sleep disturbances. For the first few weeks afterwards, I didn't have much of an appetite. I felt queasy when I was eating. Oftentimes, I felt full when I had only eaten a small portion of a meal. My sleeping pattern was also affected by my grief. I would fall asleep at my regular time but then after just a few hours would awake in the middle of the night and be unable to fall back to sleep. I also had a loss of energy for approximately one month. I felt easily fatigued and I did not feel like taking the usual daily walks with my dog. Some of these same grief reactions may have also occurred to you as a non-grandparent. This is perfectly normal. Look at the list of normal grief reactions again and reflect upon your feelings. How many of the normal grief reactions have you experienced in your lifetime? How many of these grief reactions have you experienced as a non-grandparent? What coping strategies did you use for these grief reactions at the time? What coping strategies are you currently using?

I know that hindsight is always, as they say, 20/20. Today, looking back upon my non-grandparent grief journey, I think my non-grandparent life voyage may have been easier had I sought out grief counseling.

Grief counseling provides people with an avenue to talk about their emotions. Grief counseling is intended to help people cope with loss. The loss can take many forms… the loss of a human loved one, a pet, or of a desired life experience, such as a promotion or becoming a grandparent. What occurs during grief counseling? Adikew (2020) wrote in a blog post "What is grief counseling and how does it help?" that:

> Dr. Robert A. Neimeyer, a clinical psychologist and expert in grief therapy, suggested two major steps a grief counselor is required to take while working with someone dealing with the loss of a loved one. The first step involves fostering a trusting relationship with the client to create a safe and comfortable environment

for the bereaved to openly share the circumstances of their loss. The second step, apart from actively listening to the grieving person, involves the counselor asking specific questions about the nature of the client's relationship with the deceased. If the relationship with the deceased was a difficult one, counseling would require a different approach than in a situation where there was a healthy relationship between the griever and deceased.

Now that several years have passed, I realize that grief counseling would have very likely helped me move through my grief of the loss of my anticipated grandchild more quickly, and less traumatically. Dr. Neimeyer proposes three R's of processing grief: Retelling, Rebuilding, and Reinventing our Lives (Open to Hope Foundation, 2017). I truly think that grief counseling would have aided me greatly to reinvent myself in the context of my life. I encourage you to seek out grief counseling if you are feeling any grief reactions for longer than a few weeks.

In addition to the concept of grief, it is vital to discuss what is meant by "mourning" in this chapter. According to Weiss (2008), mourning is the public display of grief. Grief focuses on the internal experiences associated with the loss. "Mourning is when you express that grief outside of yourself. Mourning is grief inside out. Mourning is showing and doing. When you cry, you are mourning. When you talk to someone else about the death, you are mourning. When you write in a journal, put together a photo display… you are mourning" (Wolfelt, n.d., p.1). Wearing mourning clothes, traditionally black in Western cultures, dates back at least to the Roman Empire. "This is when the toga "pulla," made of dark-colored wool, was worn during mourning; however, black wasn't always the color of mourning in the west. For centuries, white was worn in mourning by most. This is because white was the most affordable fabric color and one most people already had" (Carter-Lome, 2024). Public wearing of black clothing is another example of mourning.

Grieving and mourning are vastly different across various cultures and faiths around the world (illume Editorial Team, 2023). In the illume blog, key cultural factors that shape grieving are listed as:

- ▷ Religious beliefs about the afterlife and nature of the soul
- ▷ Family dynamics and gender roles for mourners
- ▷ Norms around emotional expression during bereavement
- ▷ Traditional mourning rituals and customs for honoring the deceased
- ▷ Beliefs about caring for the body of the deceased
- ▷ Accepted practices regarding funerals, burials, cremation and memorial services
- ▷ Traditions around clothing, food, and activities following a loss

I think it's important to talk about "norms about emotional expressions" during mourning. I must admit that I kept my mourning the loss of my expected grandchild a secret sorrow. I did not outwardly mourn. I think this is mainly because I was raised not to cry in public. I was brought up to believe that crying was something that you do in private to appear strong to the outside world. So, I did most of my mourning in private. Even though I cried for several days after the miscarriage, I did so in seclusion. I am a religious and spiritual person. I found that praying gave me some comfort. I prayed in silence and I prayed aloud. I prayed that I would start to feel more like myself soon. I prayed that my daughter and son-in-law would have the strength to return to their normal activities and daily routines. I prayed that they would have a child someday. Praying made me feel better and was an emotional release for me. How you mourn as a non-grandparent will be unique for you. However, I hope you find the courage to mourn in public. I encourage you to express your true feelings in safe spaces with those you love and trust. Looking back, I wish I had done a bit of public mourning.

Bereavement is defined as "the period of sadness after the death of a loved one. Grief and mourning occur during the period of bereavement. People who are grieving are described as bereaved" (The National Cancer Institute, 2024, p. 1).

Because my daughter and son-in-law's miscarriage happened suddenly, I did not have time to anticipate the loss of my grandchild. Their miscarriage hit me like a ton of bricks. I believe my period of bereavement lasted longer than one year mainly because I had no time to anticipate this loss. There were milestones on the calendar that I had to get past. This included the pregnancy due date, which was six months after the miscarriage. This date was profoundly sad for my daughter and son-in-law as well as for my husband and myself. As grandparents, we planned to rent a beach property for a few weeks in the summer and have our immediate family join us for a period of time. The summer following the miscarriage had some difficult times to get through because this type of vacation did not occur. Additionally, the summer brought about the first anniversary date of the miscarriage. How long a period of bereavement lasts will vary from person to person. This is just fine. There is nothing wrong with taking your time to go through your own, unique, personal bereavement.

Now that you are familiar with the terms grief, mourning, and bereavement, you are aware that they truly are different concepts. Understanding how they are distinct from each other will help you process through your own experience.

Sadness, or "feeling blue," is often associated with a loss. The vast majority of people who experience a loss (for example, loss of a person they love, loss of a job, loss of a home, loss of an anticipated grandchild, etc.) also experience some degree of sadness. Since sadness is "typical" and expected following loss, I will use the term sadness when I discuss feelings that are expected, normal, or typical following a loss. It is vital to discuss the difference between sadness and clinical depression in this chapter.

I experienced sadness with my grief as a non-grandparent. Even though I had fatigue and sleeping and eating disturbances following the miscarriage, these troubles were short lived. I did not have symptoms of clinical depression after the miscarriage. Someone with clinical depression has feelings that go beyond sadness. Their day-to-day life is affected by this disorder. If symptoms that accompany your sadness interfere with your daily life, you may be experiencing clinical depression. According to the National Institutes of Health (NIH), some common symptoms of clinical depression are:

▷ Persistent sad, anxious, or "empty" mood
▷ Feelings of hopelessness or pessimism
▷ Feelings of irritability, frustration, or restlessness
▷ Feelings of guilt, worthlessness, or helplessness
▷ Loss of interest or pleasure in hobbies or activities

▷ Decreased energy, fatigue, or being "slowed down"

▷ Difficulty concentrating, remembering, or making decisions

▷ Difficulty sleeping, early morning awakening, or oversleeping

▷ Changes in appetite or unplanned weight changes

▷ Aches or pains, headaches, cramps, or digestive problems without a clear physical cause and that do not ease even with treatment

▷ Suicide attempts or thoughts of death or suicide (NIH, 2021).

Not everyone who experiences depression has every symptom. Some people experience only a few symptoms, while others have many of these symptoms. Each person is unique.

Sometimes in order to not let these feelings interfere with our daily activities, it is helpful to receive guidance from a healthcare professional. Talking to a professional about your feelings during on-going scheduled visits can help you work through them. When someone is diagnosed with clinical depression, however, medications are often prescribed to help the brain get back to a more "normal" processing of the experience. If your thoughts and feelings are interfering with your daily life, please contact a healthcare professional without delay. They will determine what type of treatment plan is best for you. If at any time you are thinking about harming yourself or others, please call 911, go to the nearest emergency room, or contact the National Suicide and Crisis Lifeline at the toll free number 988. This number operates 24 hours a day, 7 days a week (24/7). The Lifeline is a national network of local crisis centers that provides confidential and free emotional support to people in a suicidal crisis or emotional distress. More information can be found on-line at: https://suicidepreventionlifeline.org/

Grief "is the price we pay for love." Grief, mourning, and bereavement are distinct concepts as described in this chapter. I hope the examples I used for each concept helps you to better distinguish between grief, mourning, and bereavement in order to help you move through your own experience with more understanding. The reflection questions that follow this chapter may help you to express some feelings you have experienced, or are currently experiencing, after a loss of any kind. You are not alone.

Reflections

Describe the differences between grief, mourning and bereavement.

As a non-grandparent, what normal grief reactions have you experienced?

Which mourning and bereavement practices did you do that were similar to mine?

What mourning or bereavement practices did you do that were different from mine?

How did you live, or are you currently living, day to day with your normal grief reactions?

Place other notes or thoughts here:

CHAPTER 6

A Theory for Everything: Theories of Loss and Grief

"What separates us from the animals, what separates us from the chaos, is our ability to mourn people we've never met." David Levithan

As I shared in the previous chapter, when I experienced grief over the loss of my anticipated grandchild, I sometimes wondered if I was "normal." So, I looked for information about loss and grief in books and on the internet. I did this because I dimly remembered theories of loss and grief I learned decades ago during my nursing education but was fuzzy on specific information about these theories. Loss and grief have been studied by researchers for decades and our understanding of loss and grief has evolved over time. I understood that grief is a normal reaction to a loss. This made me more aware of my feelings as "normal." I gave myself permission to grieve the loss of my anticipated grandchild.

I want to share some of my findings with you. I can relate to some of what these authors published about loss and grief, though not all published material was relevant to me. Maybe you will feel the same way after reading this information.

Perhaps the most well-known researcher on the topic of loss and grief is Dr. Elisabeth Kübler-Ross, a Swiss-American psychiatrist who developed a widely adapted theory of loss and grief in the 1960s. In her book *On Death and Dying* (1969) Dr. Kübler-Ross proposed five stages that terminally ill persons experience: 1) shock and denial; 2) anger, resentment, guilt; 3) bargaining; 4) depression and 5) acceptance (Kübler-Ross, 1969). A visual model of Dr. Kübler-Ross' grief theory, often called a grief cycle, is found in Figure 1.

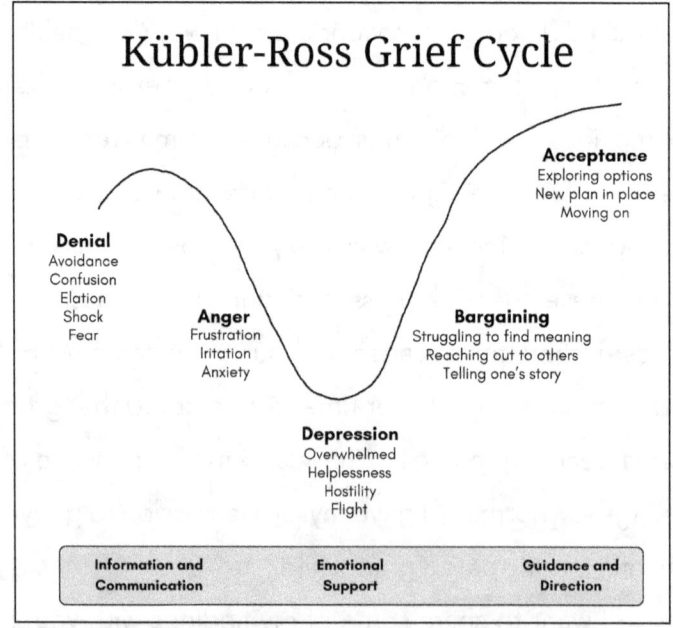

Figure 1: Based on figure provided in *On Grief and Grieving: Finding the meaning of grief through the five stages of loss,* by Elizabeth Kübler Ross & David Kessler, 2005.

Initially, Dr. Kübler-Ross proposed that individuals pass through these stages in a linear way, completing one stage and moving onto the next one. Her theory has brought an understanding of loss to those facing their own impending death or coping with the death of someone they love. However, over time, these stages have evolved. In 2005, *On Grief and Grieving: Finding the Meaning of Grief Through the Five Stages of Loss*, written by Drs. Kübler-Ross and David Kessler was published. Per Dr. Kessler's website, *On Grief and Grieving* "applies these stages to the process of grieving and weaves together theory, inspiration, and practical advice, all based on Kübler-Ross and Kessler's professional and personal experiences... the stages have evolved since their introduction and been very misunderstood over the past three decades. They were never meant to help tuck messy emotions into neat packages. They are responses to loss that many people have, but there is not a typical response to loss as there is no typical loss. Our grief is as individual as our lives (Kübler-Ross and Kessler, n.d., p. 1).

According to Hall (2011), stage theories are appealing and orderly. However, they don't represent how truly complicated grief and grieving are. Research suggests the possibility of life-enhancing personal growth, including resilience and healing, with the grief cycle (Hall, 2011). A visual model depicting grief and loss in a non-linear manner, by Dr. Evelyn de Villiers, is found in Figure 2.

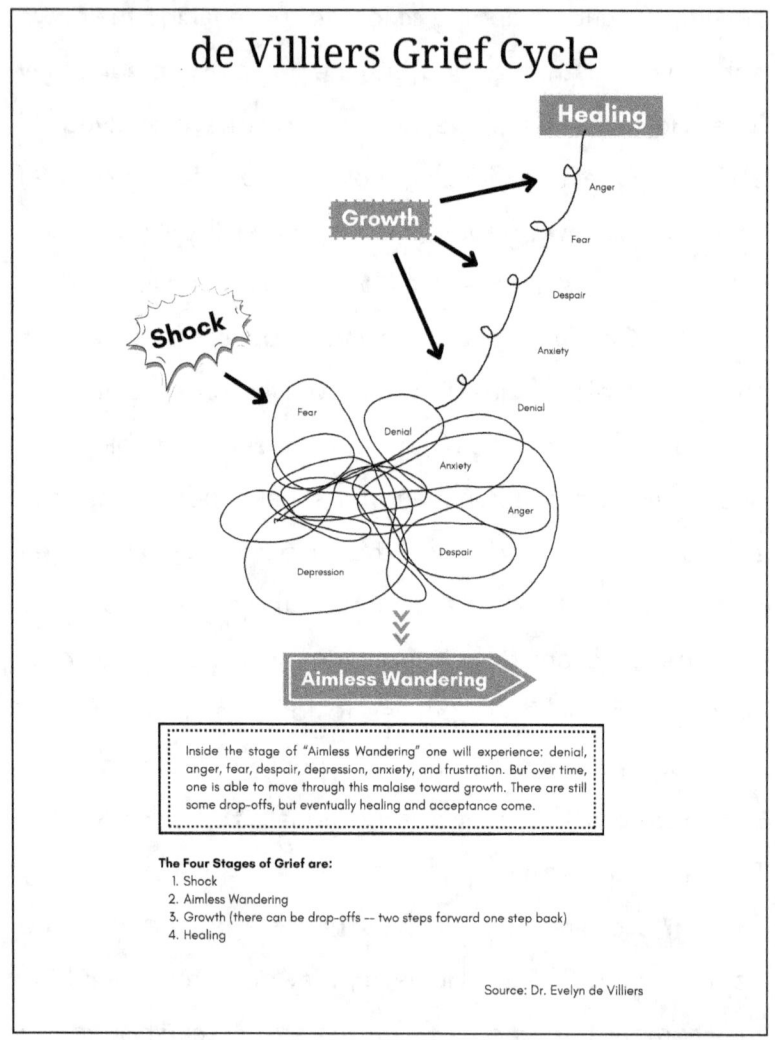

Figure 2: Garcia, C. (2014). Transformed, healed, restored blog February 20, 2014. Accessed from http://transformedhealedandrestored.blogspot.com/2014/02/grief-and-loss.html

Another viewpoint by Dr. William Worden supports grief as an active mourning process that includes four tasks: 1) acceptance of the reality of the loss; 2) processing the pain of grief; 3) adjusting to a world without the deceased; and 4) finding an enduring connection with the deceased in the midst of embarking on a new life (Worden, 2018). Dr. Worden's first three tasks are not linear; you can move forward or backward between these tasks over time. The fourth task is a task that you take on "gradually as you create a balance between remembering the person who died and living a full and meaningful life" (Our House Grief Support Center, 2022).

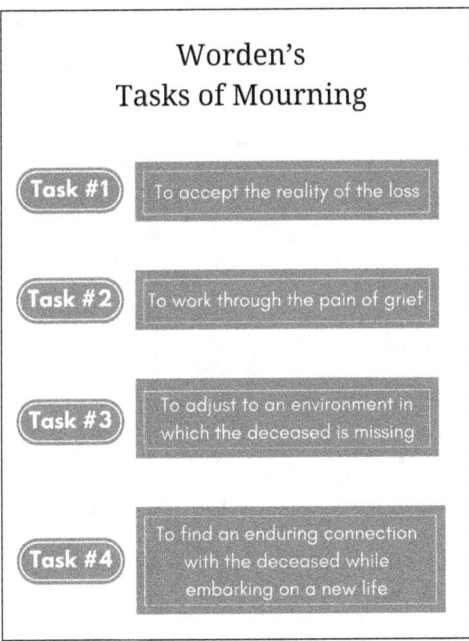

Figure 3: Worden, W. (2018). Grief Counseling and Grief Therapy: a handbook for the mental health practitioner 5th edition. Springer Publishers.

Grief is also depicted as a period of pure chaos. Since grief comes in waves, and differs from person to person, it may be chaotic for some. A depiction of the chaos that can accompany grief is also found in the visual diagram in Figure 4.

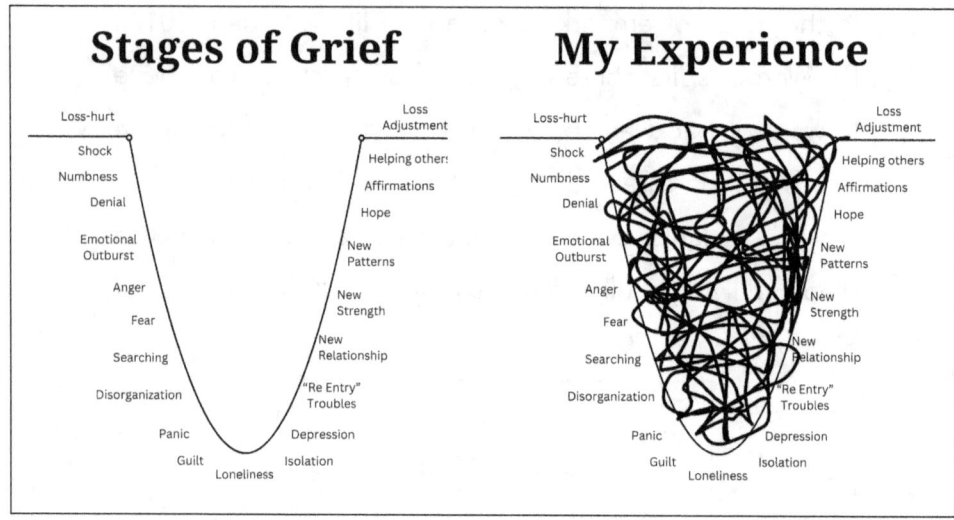

Figure 4: Based on a commonly used graphic to showcase personal experience moving through grief.

As a non-grandparent, you may be able to relate to one, or more, of these visual models. I know I have not experienced my grief as a non-grandparent in a linear manner such as depicted in Dr. Kübler-Ross' original model in Figure 1. My grief experience was not orderly. Some days were good days where I felt like myself. Other days were days where I felt a lot of fluctuations in my emotions. Some days were really painful days (rarely, but these did occur).

Most often, I felt my grief experience like the models shown in Figures 2 and 3.

Looking at de Villiers Modal (Figure 2) I experienced the four components of shock, aimlessness, wandering, grief, and healing after the loss of my desired grandchild. There were many times in the initial months where I felt like I was taking one step forward and two steps backward in my emotions. Most nights I could sleep through the night, but then I would have several nights in a row where I only slept a couple hours. Most days I could eat my normal meal portions but then on some days I had a queasy stomach and could not eat very much. I particularly remember feelings of anger and anxiety. For instance, I felt angry when I heard news reports about parents who had allegedly killed their newborn, toddler, or young child. How could someone take another's life... especially the life of an innocent child? I felt some anxiety when I wondered if I would ever be a grandparent. As a non-grandparent, you may have felt this way too. Looking at de Villiers Model again, by putting into place communication and self-care strategies that I describe in this book, eventually I reached a point of acceptance and lifetime healing.

I remember looking at the visual depiction of the Tasks of Mourning in Worden's Model (Figure 3) several times the first time I saw it. I believe that the tasks of mourning Worden describes are a natural "fit" for a non-grandparent. Being a non-grandparent can be due to any of the reasons I discussed in Chapter 3. The terms "loss" and "deceased" in Worden's tasks can be applied to the loss of a desired or an actual grandchild.

I could really relate to Worden's tasks as I remembered going through each of these tasks after the loss of my anticipated grandchild. I think it took me a few weeks to accept the reality of the miscarriage. Working through the pain of the grief took a bit longer because my daughter's due date was six months away and I had trepidation as her due date approached. Once the pregnancy due date had passed, I began to adjust more to the fact that I was not going to have this grandchild. But sometimes I felt like I was going back and forth between working through my grief and adjusting to the loss. This happened to me when I would hear about the birth of a new grandchild that a family member or friend announced.

If I were to re-draw Worden's model, I would place arrows that flowed between the tasks pertaining to working through grief and how those involved are adjusting to the loss (see Figure 5). After my daughter's miscarriage, sometimes I felt that I had adjusted to the loss and then something would occur that required me to work through my grief again. For example, I would be feeling more like myself and then someone would tell me their exciting news... they were going to be a grandparent! I would then feel some sadness about being a non-grandparent. I believe it is really true that "we can mourn people we haven't met."

It probably took me a full year to embark on my life as a non-grandparent. Over time, I felt like I was getting stronger, and more like "myself." I moved forward with the baby steps that I discuss in an upcoming chapter. But I have

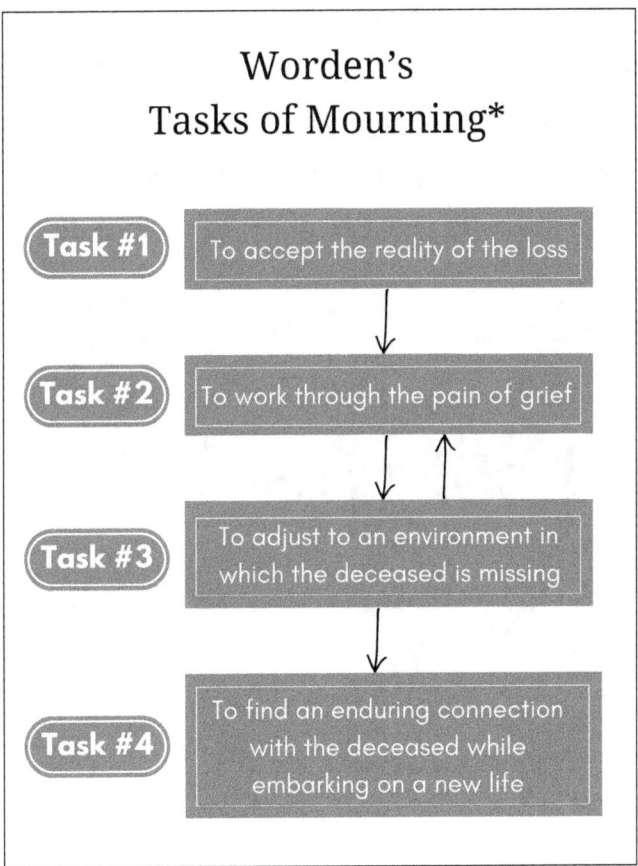

Figure 5: Author's adaptation of Worden's Model of Grief, 2018.

also had some really sad and chaotic days where I felt like the chaos image of grief as shown in Figure 4. My feelings about being a non-grandparent fluctuate, depending on what is going on in my life at the time. Over time, I have felt less like I was experiencing chaos (Figure 4) and more like I am completing tasks towards embarking on a new life (Figure 3). Have you ever felt like this has happened to you?

You may feel like your emotions fluctuate over time. Please remember that everyone grieves differently... there is no "one size fits all" approach to grieving. Give yourself permission to grieve your non-grandparenting sorrow. You deserve the right to grieve this lost life experience.

Reflections

After reading about some of the different grief theories and looking over the models, does any specific model apply best to your grief experience as a non-grandparent? Why?

I believe it is encouraging to know that grief eventually moves beyond the early stages and phases of grief. Where do you think you are now at this point in your life with your grief?

Place other notes or thoughts here:

CHAPTER 7

Let's Play Ball: Fielding Personal Questions About Grandparenting

"It's better to know some of the questions than all of the answers." James Thurber

arlier in this book I talked about how I got up the courage to speak about my "secret sorrow" regarding my being a non-grandparent to my close family and friends. The communication strategies I discussed, and now use routinely with close family and friends, have gotten better over time. I am more at ease speaking to those I love and trust with my feelings.

However, there are other people with whom discussing my "secret sorrow" is a bit trickier. It took a while for me to feel comfortable discussing my non-grandparent sorrow to someone other than a close family member or friend when <u>they</u> brought up the subject of grandchildren. I think this was largely due in part to the fact that I don't ask personal questions to other people. I am not someone who is nosy and pries into other people's business, even to my closest family and friends. So, I found questions about my personal family business unnerving. Perhaps you also feel this way when people ask personal questions.

Over time I realized that not everyone is as sensitive to other people's privacy as I am. I found that people routinely ask me, and others, very personal questions including questions about grandchildren. So, I had to start to open up about my feelings about being a non-grandparent to others. Now I respond directly and honestly to those people. It took me quite a long time to feel comfortable... it was couple years before I felt comfortable opening up to them. This was the timeframe it took for me. Your timeframe may be shorter or longer. Over time you may find that you can start to open up to those people with whom you are not really close to about your "secret sorrow."

But, how much I reveal about my feelings depends on who is asking me questions, and where we are (in a public versus a private location). This chapter details strategies I now use when questions come up regarding being a non-grandparent with those people other than my closest family and friends. I hope that some of the strategies I use will be helpful to you.

It has been my experience that family, friends, co-workers, and sometimes strangers at the grocery store ask very personal questions. I have been asked questions about grandchildren many times. More often than not, this has made me feel uncomfortable. Or sometimes it's not a specific question about grandchildren that makes me feel uncomfortable. Sometimes a conversation with a grandparent involves emphatic statements about their grandchildren or how wonderful it is to be a grandparent. Remember the instance I disclosed about the Christmas Eve encounter in my church with a grandmother? This brief conversation with a complete stranger made me realize just how important it is to be prepared ahead of time, in as many situations as possible, for questions I have a hard time answering.

Every time someone took me off guard with questions about grandchildren, I fumbled over my response. Afterwards I wished I had come up with a better reply. I would think about the question and say to myself: "Why did you say that? Why didn't you just say…" I said to myself that if someone were to ever ask me that question again, I would quickly say "my pre-determined response." I even practiced saying my responses aloud while in front of a mirror to watch my non-verbal facial expressions. This really helped me prepare for future questions from anyone… family, friends, co-workers, and even strangers about grandchildren.

It might be helpful to you to recall some personal questions you have been asked about being a grandparent. Pause and think about some of these personal questions now. How did you respond at that time? What response would you give to the same question today? These newer responses can work as possible replies the next time you are asked questions about grandchildren. You can't possibly be ready to respond to every question you may be asked. However, based upon your past experiences, you can anticipate some types of questions about grandchildren and be prepared ahead of time <u>in a way that works best for you</u>.

I believe we should be prepared to answer questions about being a non-grandparent just like we need to be prepared when a storm with heavy wind and rain is coming. We should anticipate possible questions from family, friends, co-workers, and others about grandchildren. Some questions might be so personal that we would never think of asking the same question to someone else. But not everyone thinks like we do. I'm sure you have been in another circumstance, such as a health crisis, and you are asked personal questions about this life event that you would never ask someone else. I know this happens, because it happened to me.

So, what can you do if you are not ready yet to open up to others when they ask you questions about grandchildren? I know my responses to questions about being a grandparent and/or grandchildren depends mainly on three factors:

1. Who is asking the question?

   Consider these factors: Is the question coming from a family member/friend you see regularly? A family member/friend you rarely see? A neighbor that is merely an acquaintance? A co-worker you consider a friend? A co-worker you hardly know? Somebody other than these persons?

2. Where is the question being asked?

   Consider these factors: Are you in a private location? Is this private location your home or their home? Are you alone with this person in this location? –OR– Are you somewhere out in public? Where is this public location? If you are in a restaurant, are you at a private far end table or at the center of the restaurant? Are you at a noisy bar? At a park? At your workplace (alone) or at your workplace surrounded by others?

3. How is the question being asked?

   Consider these factors: Is the questioner showing genuine concern for you? Does he/she just appear to be nosy? Is it somewhere in between both of these possibilities?

You too may feel that some, or most, of these factors that I take into consideration also apply to you when discussing personal things with others, including grandchildren. You are the best judge of when, with whom, and where you will feel comfortable disclosing your "secret sorrow" associated with being a non-grandparent.

To this day, whenever an acquaintance or stranger asks me questions about grandchildren I respond that I don't have a grandchild and then I quickly change the subject. For me, changing the subject is the easiest path for me to take with them because it is the route that is the least emotionally draining for me. I don't feel the need to inform a stranger or an acquaintance anything that is my personal business.

So, let's imagine that you are not ready yet to disclose your sorrow to people you do not consider close relatives or friends. How should you respond to their inquiries about grandchildren?

One method that works very well for me is something I call STATING and CHANGING. I answer their questions by stating a brief response and then changing the subject. This technique may be useful to you also when someone you are not close to asks personal questions, about grandparenting... or about any subject for that matter!

Some examples of personal questions and statements I have received from strangers or acquaintances about grandchildren are found in the table below. I also include some responses that I used that were helpful for me at the time. You might also find these responses, or a variation of these responses, helpful for you when you are not ready yet to disclose your sorrow when someone asks you about grandchildren.

Possible Questions/Statements	Possible Responses
Do you have any grandkids? –or– How many grandkids do you have?	Right now I don't have a grandchild. If I ever do have one I will be thrilled! Then change the subject.
Mary and John have been married for a while now... when are they going to get around to making you a grandfather/mother?	I really don't know. I think this subject is too personal/too confidential to ask them about. Then change the subject.
I read that some infertility treatments are now being covered by insurance. Do Mary and John know about this?	They have not discussed any treatment plans with me. I think this subject is too personal/too confidential to ask them about. Then change the subject.
It's been a few months since Mary had her miscarriage. Is she trying again?	I don't know. I think trying for another pregnancy is her choice when the right time comes. Then change the subject.
I heard that adoptions are not as expensive as people think. There are even grants available to help with the costs. Do you think Andy and John will go the adoption route?	They have not discussed adoption with me. I think this is a very personal decision for them. Then change the subject.
Oh... that's a shame you aren't a grandmom/grandpop yet. It is the very best thing that ever happened to me!	I have heard other people say this too. If this happens in my family I will be thrilled! Right now this subject is too difficult for me to talk about. Then change the subject.
You'll be a nana/pop-pop real soon... I can just feel it!	Thanks. Right now my feelings are in a state of flux so I appreciate us talking about something else today. Then change the subject.

Redirecting the conversation helps me a great deal of the time so I routinely use this method when someone I don't feel close to asks me any type of personal questions. This gets the "questioner" off the subject of my personal life/my grandchildren/their grandchildren and onto another subject. It works the majority of the time, for most questioners. Every now and then I encounter an annoying someone who asks the same question again even after I have changed the subject. If this happens to you, you may have to repeat your response and also add "this subject is too personal for me to talk about today. I ask for your understanding." If the annoying person still doesn't stop asking personal questions, be prepared to be very frank and tell them that this conversation is over. Also... don't feel guilty if you need to tell someone "this conversation is over" if they continue to be persistent in asking personal questions after you have expressed your feelings to them and changed the subject. You have told them your feelings on the subject. They don't get it so the conversation is over. Period.

Additionally, sometimes the questioner is not a complete stranger, but a family member, friend, or co-worker who appears to be prying into my personal business. I may get the impression from their questions that they are not genuinely concerned but are nosy. To my advantage, I may know a little bit about their personal interests. This helps me to change the subject and redirect the conversation onto a topic that is an interest of this person. This strategy focuses on doing three main things:

1. Acknowledge their question.
2. State your feelings.
3. Redirect the conversation.

Some examples of responses I found helpful for redirecting the conversation about grandchildren and/or being a non-grandparent are:

Possible Question/ Statement	Personal Interest of Questioner	Possible Redirection Response
When Is Mary finally going to give you a grandchild?	Gardening	That's a hard question for me. I think that Mary's life choices are her personal decisions. I saw that the weather channel predicted a good year for roses this summer. What are your plans for your garden this summer?
I heard that more people are using surrogates now. Are Andy and John looking into this?	Traveling	I've heard that too. I believe that surrogacy is a personal decision for couples. I heard that you were planning a trip out West soon. Tell me about the National Parks you are planning to visit?
Just wait til you're a grandparent! It's the most wonderful time of your life!	Golfing	That's what grandparents tell me. Until that happens to me it's hard to imagine these feelings. How's your golf game going? I know you played some new courses recently. Tell me about your new favorite course!

Over time, you will find that your responses may come more quickly and with more ease. The more you practice responding to possible questions, the quicker your responses will come. I encourage you to practice in advance. You will discover how to acknowledge the question, acknowledge your feelings, and then redirect the conversation. Over time, you will find what works best for you.

I certainly do not "know all of the answers." It is important to reiterate that there is no "one size fits all" approach to answering personal questions or engaging in conversations about being a non-grandparent. Your responses may depend on factors such as: Who is asking the question? Where is the question being asked? Is the questioner showing genuine concern for you?

Remember, people are not sensitive to our non-grandparenting sorrow because we tend to keep our sorrow to ourselves... from people we know well and acquaintances. Only you can judge when the time is right to discuss your sorrow with anyone. You'll begin to feel more at ease answering questions and letting others know that you are hurting regarding the fact that you are a non-grandparent <u>when the time is right for you</u>. Give yourself all the time you need.

Reflections

Who are some of the people who have asked you questions about your grandparenting status? (Use initials if you feel more comfortable)

Think about some of the questions or comments you have heard from these people already. List some of these questions or comments here.

How would you respond to these same questions or comments today now that you have reviewed some suggestions in this chapter?

Place other notes or thoughts here.

CHAPTER 8

Life Goes On:
Living with Routine Encounters
as a Non-Grandparent

"Life is a succession of lessons which must be lived to be understood." Helen Keller

*L*iving day-to-day as a non-grandparent in a grandparenting world goes beyond learning and using new communication skills to respond to questions about grandchildren. I encounter other situations as a non-grandparent on a regular basis that can evoke some sorrow. These situations vary from being invited to celebratory events, such as a baby shower, to seeing and responding to social media postings. You most certainly are faced with similar situations in your daily life as a non-grandparent.

Over time, I have found several strategies that work for me in various situations. My approaches evolved in a trial-and-error way. Sometimes an approach I used that worked well in the past backfired for me the next time I used it. I want to offer you examples of strategies that have worked for me most of the time to handle situations that came up for me regarding grandchildren. You may have encountered some of these same situations, or different ones entirely. The situations I've listed can't be put in order of importance. Each circumstance is unique. So, I've placed my personal experiences as a non-grandparent and how I respond in these situations in alphabetical order below. The strategies I suggest may work for you too.

ANNIVERSARY DATES

Anniversary dates occur annually. If your only child died, your anniversary loss of their passing is also a stark reminder that you will never be a grandparent. In other cases, when your child has experienced a loss, their anniversary date is also a loss for you. This loss can be a miscarriage, death of an infant or older child, or even the loss of a planned pregnancy due to a failed infertility procedure. Some examples of anniversary dates are a pregnancy "due date," the anniversary date of a miscarriage, the delivery date of a baby who did not survive, or the annual date that a grandchild of any age passed away. If you had a grandchild that passed away at any time, their birthday is also an anniversary date. Certain dates, such as a pregnancy "due date" or a grandchild's birthday are anticipated to be times of joy. For non-grandparents, these dates are sharp reminders that pregnancy, childbearing, and/or child rearing did not go as planned. Anniversary dates are especially difficult for me. These dates may also be especially difficult for you.

I do my best to support my daughter and her husband on the anniversary date of their pregnancy loss and on the due date of their pregnancy. The first year I visited with them on both dates to give them a hug. Now I send them a "thinking about you" card or a phone call each year. They tell me that these caring expressions let them know that I have not forgotten about their loss of Phoenix. In reality, I will never forget their loss. These dates are sad days for me. My grandchild would now be ten years old. I imagine what a child of this age would look like, be doing developmentally, be interested in, etc. You may also have these feelings if your awaited grandchild was lost due to any cause.

The main focus of a painful anniversary date should be on the person, our sons or daughters, who are experiencing this anniversary day. However, we are also affected by the anniversary date and have sadness for our children, as well as for ourselves. This sadness is for what was and for what was meant to be. This is a double-edged sword. On an anniversary date we also need to be supported. Talking with a close family member or friend about feelings prior to the anniversary date, or on this date, is vital to do. I find comfort in talking about my feelings on anniversary dates with my husband and my closest friends. You may find this helps you get through an anniversary date too.

BUMPING INTO PEOPLE

Another situation that presents a challenge to me is when I randomly "bump into someone" I know, but I have not seen recently. This has happened to me many times, at different places... a restaurant, the mall, in church, or even the grocery store. I know from experience that this encounter will lead to questions about my children and if anything is new in my family. This is only natural when someone hasn't seen me for a while. More often than not, at my age, the conversation goes in the direction of grandchildren. Sometimes it is because the person I run into gives me an update about their grandchild/grandchildren. Sometimes it is because the person asks me questions about impending grandchildren. Are you able to relate to this?

Whether I stop to chat with this person or not depends mostly on my mood on that particular day. It also depends on the setting that we are in. If I feel comfortable conversing with this person if they inquire about grandchildren I open up and am honest about my secret sorrow. I do so using the techniques I already discussed in the previous chapters of this book. Or, if I feel that I can't discuss my personal life on this occasion, or in this particular setting, I sometimes use a quick excuse and move on.

A quick excuse I use is: "We haven't seen each other for such a long time! We have a lot to catch up on. Right now isn't good since I am really pressed for time. Let's catch up later in the week by phone- or- over coffee." This gives me a way to get out of an unexpected conversation when the timing is not right for me to speak about myself and my family. Like most people, I am usually pressed for time, so I am not fibbing. Saying "I am pressed for time" prevents me from making things up such as: "I'm late for a doctor's appointment" or "I have to get home to let the dog out." I am just saying that I am pressed for time today.

You may have also experienced these types of encounters. You may already use some particular strategies to get out of having a conversation with someone you are not comfortable speaking with about yourself or your family. Or, you may feel comfortable discussing personal matters with this person, but just not today. Or maybe you just don't want to talk to someone about your family due to the physical setting you are in at this particular time. Many factors come into play in deciding with whom, when, and where you feel comfortable discussing personal things. You are the best judge of how comfortable you are talking about your feelings to any person, in what place and at what time. Trust yourself.

HOLDING A BABY OR CHILD

Fortunately, I can honestly say that, so far, no-one has asked me to hold their baby or young child. But this might not be your experience. My friend Sharon told me this situation she experienced:

> "I went to a Christmas party for my husband's company. A girl that worked in his office had a baby and asked me if I wanted to hold him. Of course I did! When I asked how old he was, he was the same age that my grand-daughter would be had she lived. I couldn't get away fast enough. I thought my heart was going to break! How I politely extricated myself I am not sure. The moment took my breath away!"

I think it is important that you know that this type of situation may happen to you. It is your right to decline to hold a baby or young child. Prepare how you will handle this situation ahead of time. Perhaps a statement such as "Julie's baby would be about her/his age now. I am not ready to hold a baby just yet. I know you will understand." Also, if you have to walk away from whatever setting this occurs in, that is your right too. You need to protect yourself.

INVITATIONS

Many of my family and friends are having grandchildren. I have been invited to their various family celebration events, including, baby showers, a child's birthday party, or a religious service such as a bris or a christening. This has most likely happened to you too.

Each invitation is unique. Again, only we can decide whether or not the timing is right to attend any of these events. What makes invitations challenging is that we have to make a decision to accept or decline the invitation by a certain deadline RSVP date.

In the past, I sometimes made up an excuse that was not completely true when responding to one of these invitations. I must admit that on more than one occasion, I told someone that I could not attend a baby shower using an excuse such as: "the date is the same day as my great Aunt Anna's 80th birthday party." I responded in this way because I was uncomfortable saying that a baby shower was too emotionally difficult for me to attend at that time.

Now that I am more comfortable discussing my feelings as a non-grandparent, I don't decline every event that involves a grandchild. I am honest about my secret sorrow. When accepting an invitation I tell the sender that I may arrive later or leave early. I have found that when someone knows about my feelings about being a non-grandparent they are supportive.

I also inquire in advance about who else will be in attendance. I then enlist someone I am close to as my "party buddy" when I attend an event that centers on a baby or a grandchild. They understand that it may be difficult for me to "ooh and ahh" when all the gifts are being opened. My "party buddy" sits with me during the gift opening and when we eat. We talk quietly about topics other than just babies and grandchildren. I usually have a better time than I anticipate since I have a support person by my side.

However, sometimes I will not accept certain social invitations. This happens for a few reasons. I may be invited to an event by an acquaintance and wonder why I was even invited in the first place. This is when I send a gift with my well wishes. Or, the event may be close to an anniversary date. I know in advance that this date will most likely be a difficult one. When this happens, I inform the host outright that I cannot attend their event, and why. For example, I have said: "your grandchild's one year birthday party would be emotionally too hard for me to attend because my grandchild would also have been turning one this month." I discovered that a true friend or close family member will understand my decision. If someone isn't supportive of your decision to decline a social invitation, this requires a more in-depth conversation with them about your feelings. Only you can gauge when the time is right for a longer conversation with this person.

I know that a true friend or close family member would never expect me to explain my decision or make me feel guilty. A true friend or close family member is mindful of my feelings. These are the types of people I need to surround myself with... I believe that you do too.

QUESTIONS, QUESTIONS, AND MORE QUESTIONS...
hold the guilt

I have told my story about some scenarios that have happened to me when questioned about a grandchild/ grandchildren. My friend Lilly told me that she has often felt guilty having to "explain" to others why she didn't have a grandchild. Lilly bravely told her story to me so I could share it:

> "My daughter has been married 15 years and neither she nor her husband have ever wanted children. When someone would ask me if she has children, and I told them "no," of course they would ask why. I explained that they didn't want children (should I even have to do that?) and the reaction was "Oh, that's so selfish to not want to have a child!" I used to counter with "Isn't it better to not have a child if that's what you want, than to have one because society tells you it's your obligation?" My guilt at being a non-grandparent went into overdrive during those times."

I frequently felt just like Lilly. I felt like I had to explain to others that my daughter has infertility issues. Usually, this led to additional questions from others about "what type of infertility problem does she have?" Or, "There are so many advances with infertility treatments now... have they considered in-vitro?" And more, and more questions. These questions did not come from my close family and friends. They did not pry. The personal questions came from other friends, co-workers, acquaintances, and even strangers. I too experienced feelings of guilt sometimes when I felt backed into a corner and had to explain why I was not a grandparent. Over time, I learned that I owe no explanation to anyone about my grandparent status. You may also be able to relate to Lilly's story. It may take you some time to feel comfortable telling a nosy person that they are asking personal questions that are none of their business. Try changing the subject. If they persist, you may have to immediately end the conversation. You may have to walk away. You need to do what works for you to avoid guilt feelings about not having a grandchild. You also must not feel guilty about changing the subject, ending the conversation or walking away. You have to protect yourself and your feelings.

SOCIAL MEDIA

Social media are part of daily life. Routinely when I use my devices I see information from family, friends, neighbors, and co-workers that include updates about grandchildren. It is sometimes tough for me to view picture after picture and posting after posting of grandparents and grandchildren. This may also be tough for you to see.

On most days I can fully read postings on social media that pertain to grandparents and grandchildren. Most days I can also write comments back to whomever has posted information. But then there are times of the year when this is difficult for me to do. The most challenging times for me to view social media postings are when families and children tend to spend more time together and appear to be having a lot of fun adventures. The specific times are Halloween, Christmas holiday time, and family vacation postings during the summer months. Ultrasound photos are also sometimes hard for me to view.

Sometimes I need to scroll quickly through social media postings about grandchildren. On some occasions I cannot read the comments that even close family and/or friends have written about their grandchild/grandchildren. Sometimes, I can look at one or two updated photos, but not all forty-five photos posted about the extended family's vacation at the beach. I then go back in a couple of days when I can emotionally look at all the new updates. I review social media postings related to grandparents and grandchildren at a pace that works for me. I do this to protect my emotions on a day-to-day basis. I remind myself that I lived my life without social media for decades before it came into existence. Another strategy that helps me is to take a social media "break." I have taken social media "breaks" for a couple days or a couple weeks. You need to decide what works best for you regarding your review of social media postings about grandchildren and grandparents. You are your best advocate. Know it is ok to keep scrolling. You don't owe anyone a comment or reaction.

STRANGER DANGER

I mentioned before that sometimes even a complete stranger would ask me questions about grandchildren. I told my story in Chapter 1 about my Christmas Eve encounter with a stranger in my church. This encounter was actually a blessing because this woman gave me the motivation I needed to write this book. I think it's important for non-grandparents to be aware that even strangers will ask you personal questions and these questions may include questions about grandchildren. Sometimes, a stranger won't even ask you a question but will proceed to talk about their grandchildren or do something else that you did not expect. My friend Karen recently took a flight to another state to visit her family. She told me this story when she returned:

> "I was seated on the plane next to a woman who looked about my age. I do like to ask people where they have been and if they are headed home. In all my years of traveling across the country, I have heard some wonderful and some heart wrenching stories. But this time I wasn't making small talk about

anything with this woman. What I did not expect was this stranger taking out her phone and showing me pictures of her grandchildren! She told me she was traveling to visit them. I heard about each one of them. I learned what grade they were in, what their favorite activities were and more. I just politely smiled and nodded my head. I should have told her that I wished I had stories like hers to tell, but sadly, I do not. I was taken by surprise by her actions, but I was also surprised at the depth of my sadness about not having grandchildren. It often comes as a surprise since I am happy that I was even able to have children, and I am happy for others who do have grandchildren. I also think about how If I could do it over again, I would have spoken up about my feelings. It all just happened so fast. I feel like now I have to keep my guard up when traveling, although I will also miss those other types of wonderful stories too."

If you felt uncomfortable, or sad, if a similar circumstance happened to you, please know you are not alone in your feelings. You are now aware that, like Karen, you have to keep your guard up even around strangers. Even though you wouldn't pull out your phone and show personal photos to others without asking if they are interested in seeing them, not everyone has your sensitivity. We can't control others' behavior, but we do have control over our responses to it.

TALKING, TALKING, AND MORE TALKING ABOUT GRANDCHILDREN

In Chapter 4, I told my story about how I finally found the courage to speak up about my non-grandparent sorrow. In Chapter 7, I gave examples of how to answer questions about grandchildren... even questions from strangers. Oftentimes, a routine situation that non-grandparents experience is when a grandparent talks incessantly about a grandchild/grandchildren. By this I mean talking, talking, and more talking by a grandparent that just goes on and on. Using the techniques I reveal in Chapters 4 and 7 to sensitively let someone know that you are a non-grandparent is imperative.

A next step could be informing them that you are interested in hearing about their grandchild, but also that you would like to discuss other things over lunch. Non-stop talking about a grandchild may make you feel worse around an anniversary date (as mentioned in this chapter) or during the holiday season. For me, anniversary dates and the holiday season are the times of year that I find it hardest to listen to never-ending stories. Joann told me her story about her feelings during the holiday season:

> "Both my husband and I have difficulty dealing with friends when they talk constantly about their grandkids. While we are interested in hearing about them, it can be hard, especially at the holidays. Christmas is the hardest time for me because there is

so much emphasis on extended family. I have thought about going away for Christmas but would never do it because our adult children wouldn't understand. Sometimes our friends don't realize why we travel as much as we do but I hesitate to say "Because we don't have the activities that you do with your grandkids. Maybe I will muster the courage to say that sometime."

Her husband added:

"The most challenging situations occur when friends talk constantly about their grandchildren because it inadvertently highlights our non-grandparent status. I think that this is particularly difficult for my wife because in our circle of friends, we are the only non-grandparents. This has been exacerbated in the past few years since we moved into a 55+ community."

You too may live in a 55+ community and be surrounded by many grandparents. Non-stop talking about grandchildren may happen to you even more often than questions about grandchildren occur. Before I learned how to speak up about my non-grandparent sorrow to others, the non-stop talking by grandparents was painful for me to bear. But I never told these people that I was having a hard time listening to their stories. So, they had no clue that their stories were difficult for me to hear. Once I spoke up about being a non-grandparent, and my feelings about being a non-grandparent, I found that people were supportive of me and my feelings.

VARIOUS OTHER CIRCUMSTANCES

There are also other circumstances that have happened to me regarding grandparents and grandchildren that I believe are important to mention. These are not in any particular order of how often they have happened to me or how important I think each of these are. I placed these circumstances together since they do not "fit" into a category previously discussed. I include strategies I use when I encounter these situations. These strategies may be ones you have already used in your encounters. Or, you may find some of my suggested strategies new suggestions for you to use.

1. Sending out a congratulations card in the mail

I have always believed it is important to acknowledge exciting things that happen in families. For as long as I can remember, I have routinely sent out congratulatory cards for engagements, weddings, graduations, new homes, retirement, and also for pregnancies and the arrival of a new baby. As a non-grandparent, I continue this practice for new babies. However, it is sometimes difficult for me to read the sentiments found in congratulatory cards for pregnancies and new babies.

One strategy I now use is to purchase different types of cards in advance to have on hand. When it's a good time emotionally for me to go card shopping, I stock up on congratulatory cards for pregnancy, baby boy, baby girl, and new grandchild events. This can be costly in dollars, but this shopping strategy helps me in the long run. Then, when someone has a baby event that I want to acknowledge, I already have the card at home. Since I read the sentiment in the card at the time I purchased it, I don't even have to re-read it prior to sending it. Sometimes very sentimental cards can stir up emotions just by reading the card. Most times, I just sign the card and place it in the mail. If you are also someone who routinely sends out congratulatory cards in the U.S. postal mail, try this strategy of buying cards in advance and not re-reading them prior to mailing them out to see if this makes this gesture easier for you to do.

2. Finding yourself in the baby aisle in the grocery store or baby section in a department store

Sometimes if I am not paying attention to where I am going in a grocery or department store, or if I am in any store for the first time, I end up in the baby aisle. These aisles and store sections can be difficult for me at times to be in. Maybe you feel this way too.

Until I was a non-grandparent, I never realized how darn cute babies and toddlers photos are depicted on all the merchandise for sale. This holds true for diaper boxes, food items, toys, and even medications. Clothing items in department store aisles are adorable! Depending on the day, just seeing all of these items is sometimes enough to stir up my emotions.

So how do I usually immediately respond when I find myself in this situation? If no one is right behind me, I do a quick turn around and go onto another aisle in the grocery store or another section in a department store. I then make a mental note to avoid this section in the future.

But sometimes turning around in the aisle is not possible. Sometimes due to circumstances of other people being behind or alongside me, I have to remain where I am. So, what happens next? One thing I do is I look straight ahead. I try my best to avoid looking at the merchandise. I also walk faster than my usual pace to get out of this section of the store as quickly as possible. There are other times when I feel like I can look at the merchandise. Sometimes it's a quick peek and sometimes I truly look things over. At times in a department store, I go through the articles of clothing, even going as far as picking out one or two items to look over the size and to feel the fabric. Again, it all depends on how I am feeling that day. There is no "correct" approach to use if you find yourself in a similar situation. You need to respond to looking at baby and child items in a way that works best for you at that moment.

3. Getting items in the mail such as birth announcements and family holiday cards

Sometimes my emotions take over when I receive mail containing birth announcements with pictures included and the photos that come with seasonal holiday cards. You may have experienced similar feelings when receiving these types of items in the mail.

One strategy that helps me is a mindset I have now. I look through the mail and only open those items that I can't delay opening... such as credit card or insurance statements. There is no rush to open any other mail! I sometimes save other mail items and open them later, even several days later. During the winter holiday season, I can usually tell from the shape or weight of the envelope that it is a photo card. There was a time when I saved all of the holiday photo cards and opened them all at once. I did this on a day during the holiday season when I felt emotionally strong enough to do so. It was easier for me just to open these items all at once. Recently, items such as these are less difficult for me to open whenever I receive them, so I open them right away. Then again, sometimes out of the blue I will have some difficulty again and will put off doing this and save the cards to open on another day. You may find this technique helpful for you too.

You may have also already encountered some of these circumstances: anniversary dates, bumping into people, invitations, social media, and other situations. You may have experienced other circumstances that I did not address. As a non-grandparent you may find some, or all, of these circumstances to have some level of difficulty for you to cope with. You may already have handled these circumstances in a way that works out very well for you. If so, you should just go on using whatever approach works for you when you encounter certain situations. But if you find yourself struggling to act when certain situations occur, I encourage you to try one or more of the strategies I found to be helpful to me. You need to discover what works best for you depending on the specific situation you encounter. Most times, this will be through trial and error. Do not worry. This is ok. Grief/Loss is a process that is individual and you have permission to do what you need to support yourself while you move through difficult feelings.

I believe that "life is a succession of lessons." There is no exact timeframe where dealing with all this extraneous "stuff" as a non-grandparent gets easier, or, ever gets easy to do. If over time, you continue to have great difficulty attending family events with babies and young children, responding to social media posts and/or other situations you routinely encounter, contact your healthcare professional to discuss this. It is extremely important to remind you that if any situation or experience gets in the way of your normal day to day functioning, seek help. This can be by either contacting your healthcare provider or going to the nearest Emergency Room. Healthcare professionals can determine if your feelings and reactions are part of normal sadness that accompanies being a non-grandparent, or if you are experiencing clinical depression. You are very important, to yourself and to so many other people in your life. Do what you need to not let the sadness you are experiencing change you too deeply. If talking to a friend or family member isn't enough, do not feel guilty going to a professional.

Reflections

Which of the situations discussed in this chapter have also happened to you? List them here.

Look over the list you made. Which has been the most difficult for you to face? Why?

How have you responded to any of the situations you listed above?

What technique will you use the next time you come across this same situation?

List other situations you have faced as a Non-grandparent that are not found in this chapter. Include how you responded to this situation in the past. State a technique you may try the next time you come across this same situation.

Place other notes or thoughts here.

CHAPTER 9

Moving Forward with Baby Steps: Lifetime Healing and Caring for Self as a Non-grandparent in a Grandparenting World

"No sun outlasts its sunset but will rise again and bring the dawn." Maya Angelou

I don't want a crystal ball to see what my future holds for me about any part of my life... relationships, health, finances, or being a grandparent. It is possible that I may never be a grandparent as much as I long to be one. I must be realistic. Or, I may be a non-grandparent for a very long time prior to becoming a grandparent. At this stage of my life I believe a grandchild will bring great fulfillment to me. As a non-grandparent I need to find other outlets for fulfillment *and* to care for myself along the way.

I want to share with you some things that I do for self-fulfillment and to care for myself. Some of these things I have done for a long time; other things are new for me. Some of the activities I do now have changed due to the Covid-19 pandemic. For example, due to Covid-19 restrictions in 2020, I began to spend more time doing outdoor activities such as gardening and walking. Maybe some of these same things will be helpful for you too.

As a nurse, I have taken care of others for over 40 years. Early in my professional career I worked long hours, including weekends and holidays. I began to experience what is commonly called "burnout." I would dread going to work and I was not putting 110% of me into my day. This was not good for me but it was also not good for my patients and their families. I realized that to care for others I had to learn how to care for myself. This did not come naturally to me and I had to work hard at it. Where did I start?

My journey to practicing self-care as an adult began when I was in my mid-20s. Out of the blue, Carol, a childhood friend who I remained close to after college, told me that she was going to take adult ballet lessons at a local dance studio. She wanted to know if I was interested. This was something I never thought of doing on my own. I agreed to try this new adventure and off we went to purchase tights, leotards, and ballet slippers! We took ballet classes every Wednesday evening at 6PM for two years. We stopped when we both became pregnant about the same time.

My friend had a healthy baby. As I already stated earlier in the book, my first pregnancy ended with a preterm birth of my daughter Marissa at 26 weeks. She lived for eight short days in a Philadelphia neonatal intensive care unit (NICU). I lost my second pregnancy with a miscarriage at ten weeks. Both of these experiences were devastating. After my pregnancy losses I attended support group meetings with other bereaved parents. After only a couple group sessions I found that they were not helpful to me. Listening to others tell their stories of loss and coping made me feel sadder. I then found solace with one-on-one counseling with a grief counselor. My grief counselor helped me recognize that I needed to talk about my feelings about my pregnancy losses with people I was close to. My counseling also helped me realize that I had to do things to care for myself. I never resumed ballet classes, but they paved the way for me to explore options of things to do, at least weekly, to care for myself. I now understand the importance of doing something daily for self-care. But in the beginning, many years ago, doing something even weekly for self-care was beneficial for my healing.

The first thing I did for self-care after my pregnancy losses was to join a local gym. I made it a priority to go there and exercise on Saturday afternoons. After only a few sessions, I appreciated how exercising made me feel more alert and less anxious. So I began going to the gym at least three times a week. I found that being somewhere other than at work or home was what I needed to boost my energy and my spirits. Today, a gym membership is routine for many people. Over 30 years ago it was not as commonplace, especially for women. I had a gym membership for a couple years and then became pregnant again. With this pregnancy, my third, I began to bleed at ten weeks and I was placed on pregnancy bedrest. After a few weeks, the bedrest was discontinued, but I was not permitted to lift objects, do housework, or have any sexual activity. Even following these restrictions, I began bleeding again. I was placed back on bedrest for the remainder of the pregnancy. My husband and I were elated when our second daughter was born healthy at full term. Hence, her middle name is "Joy."

Our daughter was born in the summertime. The weather was perfect for taking her on long walks in the stroller. I found that while walking her I could take in the sights and sounds of nature. I started to enjoy this means of solo exercise rather than using equipment at a noisy gym. My outdoor exercise routine was short-lived when I became pregnant when our baby was nine months old. This pregnancy too required bedrest, this time due to preterm contractions. Because of the support of our family, especially our parents (the grandparents), to help my husband care for our young daughter and do household chores, our third daughter was also born healthy and at full term. Hence, her middle name is Julia, as she is our "Jewel."

Today, I do several things to care for myself. About ten years ago I discovered that having quiet time to myself each morning gave me a peaceful start to my day. My morning routine is to turn my cell phone volume to "off," pour a cup of coffee, and then sit quietly to pray for about 15 minutes each morning. Afterwards, I refrain from turning on the television for another ten minutes or so. The chaos of the world can wait. I do this same routine even when we are away from home. My husband snores (loudly). If we are staying in the tight quarters of one hotel room, I go to another location, sometimes outside the hotel, to have my quiet morning time. If we are staying in a family member's home, I set my alarm to wake earlier than others so my quiet morning routine is not interrupted.

Additionally, I do other self-care activities. Oftentimes, I just turn on music and listen to it. Sometimes, I turn up the volume loudly and dance (like no one's watching)! Like me, some people feel better by listening to music. Some people have more energy by exercising. Some prefer exercising in a formal class with other people and others prefer to exercise solo. My sister Sharon is a member of a gym that has an Olympic-sized pool. She makes the time to swim laps several times a week year-round for exercise and to recharge herself. No one way to care for yourself is perfect or works for everyone. My preferred methods are exercising and finding quiet time for myself. You may prefer self care by a special dietary practice or maybe guided relaxation or formal mediation. Have you found what self-care activities work best for you?

Today, using a treadmill is boring to me. I prefer to walk outdoors by myself, where I clear my mind and listen to sounds of nature. I feel energized when I walk 1.5 miles in the morning. I know from my previous use of a treadmill that at my comfortable walking pace of 3.2 miles per hour, it takes me 18-19 minutes to walk one mile. So, when I walk close to 30 minutes, I have walked 1.5 miles. I try to do this five mornings a week. I get bored taking the same route every day, so I change my walking pattern. I walk one way for 15 minutes then turn around and return home.

I wish I was one of those people I see out walking or running no matter what the weather is like. I must admit that when it's bitter cold, there is a gusty wind with a freezing wind chill, or it is hot and humid, I avoid walking outdoors. The community where we live has an on-site gym. I use the gym treadmill on certain days due to the weather conditions. You may find the gym too expensive for your family budget. Or you may live in a neighborhood where it is not safe to walk alone outdoors. Traveling to a local mall a few times a week to walk indoors may be an option for you to consider. Also, some workplaces have on-site gyms for their employees. Many don't take advantage of this option prior to, or after, working. You may want to consider strategies to arrive at work earlier, or leave later, so you can put exercise time into your workday. If lunchtime exercise is an option at your place of employment, carve out time in your lunch break for exercising and ask a coworker to be an exercise buddy. Exercising with a partner is oftentimes longer lasting than exercising solo. Whenever you can, get outside to walk, because nature has many healing benefits.

A newer exercise activity I enjoy now is golfing. My husband has been a golfer for decades. He encouraged me to take up this sport about ten years ago. He was wise and knew that he should not be my golf instructor, so he purchased a series of lessons for me and is my caddy instead. I have watched golf tournaments on TV for decades, first with my father, then with my husband. Until I started to learn how to golf, I never realized how frustrating this sport can be. This is primarily because I have to think about so many things when getting ready to hit a ball… proper body posture, keeping my head down, the placement of my feet in relation to where the ball is and what club I am using, standing at the appropriate distance from the ball, keeping my left arm stiff (I am right handed), and the list goes on. But now that I am getting (a little bit) better at my golf game, I am actually enjoying this sport.

There are many other ways to exercise besides dancing, walking, swimming, or a sporting activity. There is very strong evidence about the benefits of yoga to both mind, body, and spirit. Historical evidence of the existence of yoga was seen as long ago as 2700 B.C. (Ocean, 2024). Yoga is a total mind-body workout. There are more than 100 forms of yoga, some relaxed and gentle, some fast paced and intense. (Watson, 2023). According to Dr. Natalie Nevins, a board-certified osteopathic physician and yoga instructor in California, "the purpose of yoga is to create strength, awareness, and harmony in both the mind and the body... regular yoga practice creates mental clarity and calmness, relieves chronic stress patterns, relaxes the mind, centers attention, and sharpens concentration" (American Osteopathic Association, 2024).

I have participated in the gentle type of yoga classes on and off for about ten years. I have even joined a few classes when we are away on vacation and I saw an advertisement for them. I have always left a session feeling more relaxed than when I entered. The refreshment of my mind-body interaction usually lasts a few days. If you feel that yoga isn't an option for you because of your age, body type, or ability, I encourage you to contemplate the words of Kerri Hanlon, founder, co-owner and yoga teacher near Philadelphia, PA. Kerri proposes that yoga is for everyone... all ages, abilities, body shapes, and sizes. She believes the heart of a yoga practice is the art of acceptance, of ourselves and others (Yoga Home, n.d.). I encourage you not to shy away from yoga for self-care if you have not tried it!

In addition to physical exercise, meditation also has proven health benefits. Meditation practices can decrease stress and improve mood by decreasing stress reactivity on several levels… psychologically, physiologically, and neurobiologically (Pascoe et al., 2021). Research proposes that a regular meditation practice can result in moderate improvements in several health issues, including binge eating, sleep disturbances, chronic pain, diabetes, high blood pressure, and mental health (Allen, 2020).

According to Heather Stang, who has a master's degree in thanatology, the study of death, dying, and bereavement, some of the most common benefits of meditation to help with grief are:

1. Helps with sleep
2. Aids in managing physical symptoms (headaches, unpleasant feelings in chest and stomach)
3. Boosts immune functioning to stay healthy
4. Aids with mental resilience
5. Connects you more deeply to your own inner insight
6. Creates a sense of connection with others who are grieving so you feel less alone (Stang, 2018)

I practice meditation when I take a yoga class and during my morning prayer ritual. I know I would reap more positive health benefits if I carved out more time in my day to practice meditation. This is an area of improvement that I need to work on.

Ms. Stang also includes a 20-minute audio titled "Guided Meditation for Grief and Sadness" on her website that you may find helpful. The meditation aims to help individuals cope with the emotions that accompany loss. I find it helpful and you may too.

Additionally, caring for yourself also includes avoidance or limitation of certain substances. When stressed, I have a tendency to eat things in excess that I should not eat. My weaknesses are chocolate, ice cream, and carbohydrates. Popcorn and pretzels are my biggest carbohydrate comfort foods. Sometimes, I can't seem to get enough carbs! When stressed I would also have a glass or two of wine to relax. But when I drink wine I also get cravings for my comfort foods. Drinking wine and munching on carbohydrates caused me to gain weight in the past. So now I limit my alcohol use to two nights a week with a two-drink limit. Current recommendations defining moderate drinking are "up to one drink per day for women and up to two drinks per day for men" (U.S. Department of Agriculture, n.d.).

Something I also do that helps to maintain my weight is to do my oral hygiene nightly about 7PM. I brush my teeth, use the water pic, and then floss. After I take the time to do all of this, I don't want to have to re-do my oral hygiene before bed. This really works for me to refrain from eating or drinking anything afterwards. You may find that 7PM is too early for you to do your oral hygiene. But, doing it earlier than you usually do might help you avoid eating and drinking after dinner too.

Getting adequate sleep each night is also very important for self-care. Research findings are promoting at least seven hours of sleep each night for health benefits for adults. These are general recommendations, not rules (Solan, 2023). Sleep quality, or how well you sleep, needs to be considered. "If you awaken refreshed and feel like you have the energy to get through your day, then I would worry less about the exact number of hours you're sleeping," (Zhou, 2023, p.1). I try to get at least seven to eight hours of sleep nightly but sometimes it is difficult to unwind and fall asleep, especially when I feel stressed.

Some people find that reading a book in bed at bedtime is helpful for them to relax and fall asleep. I have never had this experience so I do not read prior to bedtime. I'm one of those rare persons where reading in bed actually keeps me awake! I find that drinking herbal tea with dinner helps me to fall asleep more easily. Taking a warm soaking tub bath helps me also. When I watch TV in the evening I watch game shows or comedy TV. I find that when I watch action or drama TV prior to bedtime I get wound up and I am actually wider awake. Maybe you have noticed similar influences on your nighttime routine.

I also refrain from using electronic devices for reading and online activities at least one hour prior to bedtime. I do this to decrease my exposure to blue light prior to bedtime. Blue light is a portion of the visible light spectrum that can affect alertness, hormone production, and sleep cycles. This wavelength of light is emitted by electronic devices (Newsom & Singh, 2024).

Research with children and adolescents has found that the blue light coming from electronic devices stimulates human brain activity and impacts quality of sleep. Adults are now being included in similar studies. A study done at the University of California regarding adult exposure to smartphones close to bedtime found that use of smartphones at bedtime may lead to poor sleep quality and negatively impact sleep (Christensen et al., 2016). A more recent study conducted by Harvard University found similar findings (Harvard University Publishing, 2022). Harvard researchers did an experiment comparing the effects of 6.5 hours of exposure to blue light to green light of comparable brightness. Blue light suppresses melatonin for about twice as long as green light. According to Newsome & Singh (2024), this wavelength of light is emitted by many electronic devices such as:

- ▷ Fluorescent lights
- ▷ LED lights
- ▷ Smartphones
- ▷ Televisions
- ▷ Computer screens
- ▷ Tablets
- ▷ E-readers
- ▷ Video game consoles

These authors recommend not using sources of blue light for two to three hours prior to bedtime to improve the quality of your sleep. So I need to work on increasing my time avoiding devices from one hour to at least two hours now that I know this information.

I avoid taking over-the-counter medications to help me sleep; they may help temporarily, but lifestyle changes are usually the best strategy for sleep issues. Sleep aids are not a magic cure (Mayo Clinic, 2024). If you have trouble falling asleep, or staying asleep, you need to contact your healthcare professional for an assessment and their recommendations for you.

I have long believed that in addition to caring for myself, I had to discover other avenues other than family, home, and work responsibilities for self-fulfillment. For me, giving back to the community by doing service projects brings great self-fulfillment. In college I was required to do a service project for a public health course. *Reach Out and Read* was a grant funded community program to promote literacy. It stressed the value of adults reading to young children. I went weekly to a local community clinic and read to children in the waiting room. Those of us who participated in this service activity were role modeling behavior (reading to the children) to their adult parents or guardians. Each child also received a new book when leaving the clinic after their appointment. After this experience, I looked for other opportunities to engage in service in the community.

There was a soup kitchen with a free health clinic open on weekends from 11AM to 1PM in close proximity to the urban university where I worked. This resource was primarily used by homeless persons and families on very limited incomes. Nurses were needed to do blood pressure screenings at the clinic. In 1999 I began service monthly here and on many occasions I would bring along our daughters. They would assist in the large community room by setting the tables, serving meals, and cleaning up afterwards. During the Christmas holiday season, my husband would join us. This was the time of year when donated unwrapped toys needed to be sorted according to age groups in a large auditorium. Children were supervised by volunteers as they came through the auditorium to select two toys each. Engaging in this service as a family was revealing to our young daughters regarding how fortunate they were to have a stable physical home environment with guaranteed meals each day. They learned what social justice entails and the importance of civic engagement. This served as a catalyst to engage them in routine service projects during their high school and college years. Our family speaks about the lasting impression the activities at the soup kitchen had on us personally. Our daughters' desire to continue to give back to the community as adults fills us with pride.

When we moved away from this urban area, I needed to find another service project to engage in. On two occasions, I accompanied a neighbor to deliver meals to the homebound. This service entailed dropping off a meal to one person and then driving to the next location for a meal delivery. I could easily see that some of the elders only wanted you to leave a meal at the door. But I also realized that many of the homebound wanted to chat with you when you came to their door, some even inviting us inside their home. We could only spend a couple minutes at each location, so as not to be delayed delivering meals to the next person. This was a disheartening experience for me. I thought the seniors we delivered meals to were lonely and would benefit from someone visiting with them longer. I knew this was not the service project for me.

A friend told me about a regional food bank approximately 30 minutes from my home. This agency is housed in a large warehouse and operates year-round. It primarily provides boxed foods to families with young children and the elderly. The coordinator assigns you to a three-hour shift with other people from the community and/or people from local and regional businesses. Groups of people work in teams in an assembly line fashion to package boxes with multiple non-perishable food items. When I go to the food bank I feel like I am making a difference for many people with the volume of boxes that are put together in a three hour shift. I have also done this service with health professions students I supervised during a summer internship. These students report they are enlightened about this agency and plan to continue assisting here as their schedule permits. If only one intern each summer follows up on this, I have made even a bigger impact in my region.

Then the pandemic hit with multiple shut-downs across the U.S., including the community where I live. Since vaccines for Covid-19 were still months away, and I was 65 years old, I did not feel comfortable returning to indoor activity at the food bank. Nevertheless, I knew I must continue to do a service activity not just to help a community member or organization, but to help me feel fulfilled too. Just by chance, I heard about one of my neighbors who lived alone, without family close by, and had to now use a walker for a hip issue. She needed surgery but due to the pandemic, her surgical date was put on hold. My neighbor needed help to walk her dog multiple times daily. Our neighborhood formed a dog walking schedule with myself and three other women taking turns seven days a week walking him. Eventually my neighbor had surgery with Physical Therapy for several weeks afterwards. Hence, walking the god lasted a few months. This made me feel fulfilled, and also grateful. I was grateful that at my age, my knees and hips were not bothering me and I could walk dogs at all, or just walk for pleasure outdoors on a routine basis. After this experience with my neighbor, a dear friend of mine also needed help walking her dog on a consistent basis due to health issues. I, along with another one of her friends, became one of her regular walkers.

Another way to have an impact on your community, as well as fulfill your desire to interact with children, can be found at your local elementary school. I am aware from my public health nursing experience that schools and summer camp programs need volunteers for their childrens' programs. A background check may be required, but this is a minor detail if being there gives you connection to kids while engaging in activities that grandparents do.

To care for yourself you need to find an activity that works for you... something that gives you pleasure. And, if you stop doing this activity for a while, DON'T FEEL GUILTY. You can always take short breaks and then resume again.

I have talked about things I find are helpful to me for self-care, and for self-fulfillment. Everyone is unique. Like me, trial and error will be the path that leads you to the self-care and self-fulfillment methods that will be the best choices for you. Take your time to discover what helps you care for yourself and feel fulfilled. Avoid what does not.

In closing, I want to tell you a personal story to demonstrate how small things, taking baby steps, can help you every day.

I receive many catalogs in the U.S. postal service/ mail from merchants I have purchased items from in the past and from merchants I have never even heard of. You probably do too. About ten years ago I was looking through a catalog that contained signs with specific messages. You know the type... "Kiss the Cook" or "I only golf on days that end in Y" messages. One sign really spoke to me, with colorful balloons stating: "Do one thing every day that makes you happy."

I thought to myself "Yes! I should do something each and every day that makes me happy or makes me smile." So I purchased it! I hung it in my kitchen and saw it every morning when I poured my coffee. Every day I made a concentrated effort to do something just to make me happy or make me smile. Sometimes I exercised. Sometimes I helped someone who was struggling to place items into their car in a public parking lot. Sometimes I danced like no one was watching.

When I became a non-grandparent, because of the sadness I was feeling, I stopped doing something every day for my happiness. After I started feeling more like me, I began doing something for myself every day that made me happy and this became my priority. I moved the sign to my work office at the university. Over time, many people saw it and some even commented on it. Some comments have been questioning ones, such as "do you really do that?" Many others have said to me: "that sign has a great message. We need to do something to make ourselves happy every day."

So this is my invitation to you. To heal as a non-grandparent you need to put yourself first and do something every day that makes you happy. Find a community service project that will make you feel like you made a difference. Place your time and energy into an old hobby or interest you used to enjoy. Or, be daring and take up a new hobby. It took me a while to find the service projects at the food bank and dog walking that made me smile. It took even longer for me to take up the hobby of golf to get some enjoyment, rather than just frustration, from golfing. I encourage you to make your life changes with baby steps... healing and caring for yourself is ongoing for your lifetime. The sun does not "outlast its sunset but will rise again and bring the dawn."

Non-grandparents deserve to be happy. We need to rise above our sorrow both to care for ourselves and to feel fulfilled. Give yourself permission to have a joyful life.

I wish you a rainbow after the rain in your life. We deserve our rainbows.

Reflections

What types of activities did you do in the past for self-care?

What activities do you currently do for self-care? How similar or different are they from past activities?

What have you done in the past for self-fulfillment?

What activities do you currently do for self-fulfillment? How similar or different are they from past activities?

What self-care activity or self-fulfillment activity can you try this week just to be daring?

How did this activity go? Are you going to continue it or move on to something else?

What was the most useful information you learned from this chapter? Why?

What was the most useful information you learned from this entire book? Why?

APPENDIX

Help for Family and Friends: Supporting Non-grandparents You Know and Love

"I get by with a little help from my friends."
John Lennon and Paul McCartney, released
on the Beatles album Sgt. Pepper's Lonely
Hearts Club Band in 1967.

hank you for taking the time to read this book because I think the messages it contains are also a gift to you. You may be a family member, friend, neighbor, or coworker of a non-grandparent. Maybe you are a grandparent, and maybe you are not. Yet, you are now learning about non-grandparents who are hidden in plain sight. You may be surprised to learn some, or most, of the information in this book. This is ok.

You may wonder now if you have made someone uncomfortable, or possibly even hurt someone, by questioning them about grandchildren. Or, maybe you are now wondering if you made over the top exuberant comments or shared numerous photos of your grandchild or grandchildren to a non-grandparent family member or friend. You had no way of knowing that anything you said to a non-grandparent made them uncomfortable or hurt them if they never said anything to you about their feelings. You did not purposefully hurt them. You were just excited.

You now know that there are many types of non-grandparents. You are aware of the emotional pain and "secret sorrow" that they tend to keep to themselves. You possess knowledge about loss, grief, mourning, and bereavement associated with being a non-grandparent in a grandparenting world. It is my hope that this book provides some perspective to others about how emotionally difficult being a non-grandparent is in our contemporary society.

You may have come to the realization that you know a few, or many, non-grandparents. Some are family members. Some are friends, neighbors, and/or co-workers.

Knowledge is power. Now you can make a difference by being a source of strength and support to the non-grandparents you know and love. You can support them in many ways, big and small. I have some tips to share with you based on my personal experience to get you started.

What are some of my key tips to pass along to you? What can you do to be a source of strength and offer support to a non-grandparent? Your actions can be whatever you do to help others who experience hardships or losses in their lives. I am certain that you have supported others numerous times who have lost a loved one, a relationship, a job, a home, or had some other losses. Stop and think about how you supported these people. Did you visit them? Make a phone call? Cook a meal? Send a card or flowers? These same caring gestures are helpful to non-grandparents. I know that when people who cared about me did a small thing, like a phone call (not a text message) just to say they were thinking about me, I felt supported and loved. Oftentimes, words are not needed. A simple hug, a stroke on the back, or sitting quietly with a non-grandparent who needs to feel supported in their journey are gestures that are profoundly helpful and genuine.

Now that you are aware of the silent grief and secret sorrow that non-grandparents have, try not to be upset by their responses, or lack of responses, to you regarding your grandchild(ren). For instance, if they turn down an invitation to a baby shower for your expected grandchild, you now have some understanding about why they declined the invitation. Refrain from inquiring as to why they can't attend. I truly appreciate it when someone does not question me as to why I can't be present at an event I was invited to. Over time I have attended more and more family events that involve grandchildren. But still sometimes I still feel the need to protect my feelings and decline an invitation. Please don't take a declined invitation as a personal insult.

When you post pictures or information on social media about your grandchild(ren) don't be surprised if a non-grandparent does not write any comments to you. Today might be a tough day for them and they need to scroll through social media quickly. They may be able to post comments later. Or, they may never comment on a particular social media posting involving a grandchild. I have seen social media postings with grandchildren too many times to count over the years. Sometimes I can respond with a comment to the writer and sometimes I cannot.

Photos of family vacations at the beach, Halloween, and Christmas time are the most difficult pictures for me to comment on. This is because these are the fun, family activities that I envisioned spending with a grandchild at this point in my life. The non-grandparents you know may feel the same way. Don't be offended by their lack of written commentary back to you. The same holds true if your family routinely sends out holiday photo cards with the grandchild(ren) included in the holiday photo. Don't be offended if you do not receive a text message or phone call about how beautiful the photo card is from the non-grandparent who received it. I sometimes must delay opening the holiday cards I know are photo cards until a time when I feel that I can view these family photos. Maybe the non-grandparents you know must do the same.

When you are together in person with a non-grandparent, don't be surprised if they change the subject after a short time if you are talking about your grandchild(ren). This may be because they are not ready yet to talk about their sorrow. Or, it just may be a rough day for them and difficult for them to hear your stories. Avoid probing by questioning. Maybe they just heard news from their son or daughter that the latest infertility treatment was not successful. Maybe their child experienced a pregnancy loss and tomorrow is the due date that they anticipated. Maybe their only child died and each time they hear a grandparenting story, it is a stark reminder, a kick in the gut, that they will never be a grandparent. There can be a number of reasons why a non-grandparent changes the subject when you are discussing your grandchild(ren). I know that sometimes it doesn't bother me to listen to grandparents talking about their grandchild(ren) and sometimes it is really hard for me to do this. It actually depends upon the day and how much information is being given to me. Try to keep this in mind if someone, even someone you feel extremely close to, changes the subject when you are talking about your grandchild(ren).

Because you read this book, you may be the one who brings up the subject of them being a non-grandparent. You may be the one who takes that quantum leap and discusses the "elephant in the room" with them. Don't worry about saying the wrong thing. Unless you blurt out something totally outrageous, such as "get over it already!" (which you would never do), nothing you say is the wrong thing to say. Another phrase to avoid (in my humble opinion) is a statement that starts out with "at least." In my opinion "at least" is a commonly used phrase that is never helpful for anyone going through a difficult time, including non-grandparents. Saying things like "at least they can try to get pregnant again" or "at least you live close to each other, and you can visit them" is not helpful at all. The phrase "at least" diminishes the intensity of the emotions that a non-grandparent feels. So, avoid using the phrase "at least" from today onward in any type of situation where you are trying to be supportive to someone.

How might you considerately begin a conversation with a non-grandparent you know and love? Start with simple statements such as "I'm sorry you're not a grandparent yet," "My heart aches for you because you will never be a grandparent," or "I'm so sorry that you aren't permitted to see your grandchildren." You can then tell them what you learned in this book. You can tell them that the concept of a non-grandparent was not on your radar screen prior to learning about this population. You can tell them that you are there for them when they are ready to talk. Your caring words may be the catalyst that helps them to open up about their feelings for the very first time. What a fabulous gift this is to the person you love!

When you are ready to get the conversation started with a non-grandparent you care about, some brief opening statements to help "break the ice" could be:

▷ You have told me that you really want a grandchild and it hasn't happened yet. I'm so sorry. You might be sad about this so whenever you want to talk, I am here for you.

▷ I am now aware that if someone wants a grandchild and doesn't have one, they tend to keep their sadness to themselves. Whenever you want to talk, I am here for you.

▷ I know you lost your only son/daughter. I now realize that your pain is doubled because you not only lost (name the child), but you lost future grandchildren. Whenever you want to talk about this, I am here for you.

▷ I know about Mary/John's (personal situation: infertility issues, miscarriage, stillbirth, child's death, failed in-vitro procedure, pursuit of career goals and postponement of having children, plans to never have children, estrangement from the family or other situation) and I didn't realize how very much this hurts you. Whenever you are ready to talk about your feelings, I am here for you.

▷ I never thought about how uncomfortable you might feel when I talk about all the things I do with my grandkids. If I have ever made you uncomfortable with my comments, I am sorry. It was not my intention.

Your opening statements may cause you, and/or the non-grandparent, to become emotional or even begin to cry. This is very meaningful. If you cry, it shows that you care about them. If the non-grandparent cries, it may be due to relief that they are now aware of your concern for them and they can now share their feelings. Try not to run away from or be ashamed of tears, because they are there to help you process your feelings. I have teared up and even cried sometimes just from emotional relief while talking to someone I love about my desire to be a grandparent and my day-to-day encounters with grandparents I know. Your first conversation may be just a brief talk, or it may be a very long encounter. Let things just flow naturally.

Conversely, your non-grandparent family member or friend may respond by saying something like "It's ok. I'm good. Don't worry about me." They may respond this way because they are not yet ready to talk about their sorrow. They may also not feel free to talk openly if you are in a public place. If this happens, just reiterate that you are there for them whenever they feel ready to talk. You may need to bring up the subject more than just one time for them to open up to you. Every non-grandparent is different and will open up to others when they are prepared emotionally to do so. Just knowing that you are there for them is most likely a huge relief to them. Sometimes, the words "I really don't know what to say but I want you to know that I am here for you" are the best words anyone can say to a non-grandparent. I know that I have found great comfort from these words said to me.

I know from my personal life circumstances the goodness of people. Whenever I experienced a loss or fell on hard times, my family, friends, neighbors, and co-workers have done many things to help me. I have received visits to my home, prayers, cards, flowers, and meals. Talking to those I am close to is comforting to me. Also, non-verbal communication says more than words could ever say. A comforting gesture to a non-grandparent can just be a hug. I am a "hugger" and I feel loved and supported when somebody just hugs me. Remember that sometimes no words are needed.

I ask you to do some homework and re-read these pages in a quiet location. Try not to have any outside distractions when reading them. The end of this Appendix has a few pages with reflection questions and space for your responses. When you have the time, please look over the questions and respond to as many as you feel you can respond to. Use your responses as the starting point for a conversation with a non-grandparent you feel close to. The first time you do this will most likely be the most difficult conversation to have with a non-grandparent. Over time, your words will come easier, and your ease with this topic will improve.

Once again, I ask you to pause to think about what people said and did when you had a personal loss or hardship of any kind. Things that you found supportive are most likely going to comfort a non-grandparent. We all "get by with a little help from our friends."

I say this with absolute certainty.

Reflections

Who are the non-grandparents you know? Use initials if it makes you feel more comfortable.

What life event made them a non-grandparent?

Has any one of them ever opened up to you about their sorrow? If so, who? How?

How will you begin a conversation to let the non-grandparent know you are there for them when they want to talk about their feelings?

How soon do you plan to initiate this conversation? Where do you plan to initiate the conversation?

How will you respond if the non-grandparent you love tells you "I'm ok, don't worry about me"?

Place other thoughts or thoughts here.

EPILOGUE

"Sometimes you have to burn yourself to the ground before you can rise like a phoenix from the ashes."
Jens Lekman

*L*iving as a non-grandparent in a grandparenting world triggered periods of sorrow for me. Depending on what was happening in my life, some periods of sorrow were shorter or longer than others. During the time I was a non-grandparent it took me quite a while to realize my feelings were justified and to feel comfortable speaking up about them. I truly believe that if I sought the help of a therapist, my time living with a "secret sorrow" would have been lessened and my quality of life enhanced. I forged ahead on my own for longer than maybe I should have.

Over time, and through trial and error, I learned how to speak up about my feelings. I also discovered how important it was for me to make time daily for self-care. The strategies described in this book helped heal my grief and live my life fully in the absence of a grandchild.

Now, my life has moved in another direction. Six years ago, my daughter and her husband adopted their beautiful, wished-for daughter. My life now is filled with the joy that a grandchild brings! I am now a "post-non-grandparent."

My time as a non-grandparent is a towering part of my life story. My memories of my time as a non-grandparent, and how I learned to navigate my journey, are forever etched in my mind. I believe this parallels my life circumstance of infertility and/or pregnancy loss. I lived through infertility and pregnancy losses. Having my "rainbow baby" after years of yearning, was a joy beyond measure, yet still bittersweet. A rainbow baby is *a baby born or adopted after a miscarriage, stillbirth or loss of an infant* (Cleveland Clinic, 2023). My living children don't, and can't, replace those that never came home. After all these years, I can still remember feelings of sadness and not being part of the "norm" when my friends, relatives, and co-workers were all having their children, yet I was not. I was also outside the "norm" when as an older adult friends, relatives, and co-workers were announcing their grandchild or grandchildren. My lived experiences helped to mold me into the person I am today. I believe non-grandparents, along with anyone living with infertility and pregnancy loss, must be supported in their life journey. My vision is that this book is a catalyst for support.

I feel it is important that readers know I am someone who looks for "signs" from a spiritual perspective. I have many spiritual signs. Rainbows, butterflies, hummingbirds, cardinals, and select musical pieces are my meaningful spiritual signs. I believe that spiritual signs are all around us.

I want to share something that occurred to me while writing this book. I enjoy listening to background music as I write. I always have the television on tuned into the *Solid Gold Oldies* channel. One day, as I was writing Chapter 9 "Moving Forward with Baby Steps" I received a tremendous spiritual sign: The song *Monday, Monday* (by The Mamas & the Papas, that I wrote about in Chapter 1) began to play on the cable channel. I stopped my writing and just closed my eyes and listened to the lyrics. This was no coincidence that this song was playing at this exact moment (May 9, 2018 at 11:47 am Eastern Daylight Savings Time). I did not cry. I paused to reflect on all that has happened in my life since July 2014 when my daughter and her husband announced their pregnancy to us. Through all the hardest times and darkest hours, I discovered family, friends, neighbors, and co-workers who were at my side. Even though I did not initially disclose to them my sorrow about being a non-grandparent, I received so much support from those I am close to after I spoke up about my silent grief and secret sorrow. I hope non-grandparents find the courage to speak up about their secret sorrow so they can get the support they need in their life journey.

I also hope non-grandparents see the signs that appear around them. You may get a similar sense of peace as I do when you are open to receiving them.

With profound gratitude,

Mary Ellen

October 2024

Email contact: nursemaryellen1977@gmail.com

do one thing
every day
that makes you
happy

ACKNOWLEDGEMENTS

I am forever grateful to my daughter Amanda and her husband Alex, who I consider my son, for their unwavering support so I could disclose my personal journey as a non-grandparent after their pregnancy loss. They are stronger than they realize. You are loved beyond measure.

The credit for keeping me focused on publication milestones for this book goes to my publisher, Heather Felty. Her visionary approach to manuscript publication is treasured beyond words. I truly believe we were meant to cross paths at this moment in my life.

I am so very grateful for the guidance from my editor, Janet Benton. She helped me fine tune key themes in this book. Her mentorship guided me during my early manuscript development and beyond.

I am so thankful for the encouragement I received from my husband Drew. He was my rock every step of the way, from reading my initial rough drafts to listening to me during some very late night conversations... his steadfast support means the world to me.

A huge "shout out" to my daughter Ashley who introduced me to Inner Peace Press. She was the beacon who pointed me in the right direction to my final destination in Heather's expert hands.

I am forever grateful for the non-grandparent contributors that made Secret Sorrow stand out as more than just my life journey. My heartfelt thanks (in alphabetical order as no story is more important than another) Joann, Karen, Lilly, Meg, Ruth, Sharon, and Tim. I truly hope I gave their stories the respect they deserve.

To Sharon and Marsha, my sister and dear friend, with whom I initially shared my "secret sorrow." These women were catalysts who helped me gain the courage to speak up to others.

I am also grateful to have had the opportunity to publish three articles about non-grandparent grief as I was writing this book. I am thankful to Sarah who referred me to the editor of *Still Standing Magazine* to explore writing an article focusing on the grief of a non-grandparent. My thanks go out to Diana Stone, the editor of *Still Standing Magazine*, who published *Silence Is Not Golden: Navigating Non-Grandparental Grief* (2019); to Janet Roberts, editor of *Grief Digest*, who published *Silent Grief of a Non-Grandparent: Why Holidays Can Be Tough Times* (2019); and, to Charlotte Sutton at the newspaper *The*

Philadelphia Inquirer for publishing *Holiday Challenges as a Non-grandparent in a Grandparenting World* (2020).

To Ashley, Cathie, Kathy and Sarah, who shared my journal articles on social media to support me as I began my writing journey for *Secret Sorrow*.

To Cathie, Joyce, Judy, Mary Lou, and Tricia, my long time friends who listened to me along the way discuss my plans for my book and who encouraged me on more than one occasion to "do it!"

To Tricia who helped me fine-tune my reference sources. Phew! Thank you so much!

To the volunteers at the Clymer Library who printed off my chapters as I sent them out for editing. I will always cherish their cheerful dispositions as they assisted me during the early writing of my manuscript.

Last, and certainly not the least, I must thank Trapper John and Lady Ariel. My fur-babies laid by my side for hours on end as I wrote and rewrote my manuscript. I never felt alone, even on cold, snowy days in the mountains. For this I am so very blessed!

DEFINITION OF TERMS

Bereaved: someone who is suffering the death of a loved one

Bereavement: the state or fact of being bereaved or deprived of something or someone

Estranged: to arouse especially mutual enmity or indifference in someone where there had formerly been love, affection, or friendliness; to remove from customary environments or associations

Grandparent: a parent of one's father or mother

Grandparenting: the activity of being a grandparent:participation in the life of one's grandchildren as a grandparent

Grief: deep and poignant distress caused by or as if by bereavement

Infertile: not fertile or productive; incapable of or unsuccessful in achieving pregnancy

Loss: the act or fact of being unable to keep or maintain something or someone

Miscarriage: spontaneous expulsion of a human fetus before it is viable (between the 12th and 27th week of pregnancy)

Mourning: an outward sign (such as black clothes or an armband) of grief for a person's death; a period of time during which signs of grief are shown

Neonatal: of, relating to, or affecting the newborn and especially the human infant, during the first month after birth

*Non-grandparent: a person who longs to be a grandparent and actively engage with their grandchild, but due to either childbearing or non-childbearing life circumstances, is not a grandparent/does not have a grandchild

*Secret Sorrow: grief and accompanying feelings of sadness that a non-grandparent has but does not communicate to anyone

*Self-care: the activity of taking care of one's own health, appearance, or well-being.

Self-fulfillment: fulfillment of oneself

Stillbirth: the birth of a dead fetus

Theory: a plausible or scientifically acceptable general principle or body of principles offered to explain phenomena

*Note: all terms are defined according to the 2024 Merriam Webster online dictionary (https://www.merriam-webster.com/) with the exception of the term "Self-care" which is defined according to the 2024 England Oxford online dictionary (https://www.oed.com/search/dictionary/?scope=Entries&q=self+care) and the terms "Non-grandparent" and "Secret Sorrow" which are defined by the author.

Additional Reflections

I believe it is important for you to perform on-going reflection of your feelings regarding non-grandparenting. It will be helpful for you to think about how you will handle possible encounters with family, friends, and co-workers, who may or may not be grandparents. Below are some questions for you to ponder in advance to better prepare yourself for living as a non-grandparent in a grandparenting world:

How will you respond to hearing "grandparenting news" the next time someone tells you they are going to be a grandparent?

How will you support your child who is unable to have children at this time when friends or relatives announce their "baby news"?

How will you respond when someone shows you the ultrasound photo or other photo of their grandchild/grandchildren?

How will you respond to social media about another's grandchildren?

How will you respond when you are invited to a friend or family member's new baby event such as a baby shower, christening, bris, or birthday party?

How will you respond to prying/personal questions about your family and grandchildren?

What is your Plan B for all of the above?

How will you care for yourself as a non-grandparent in a grandparenting world as time goes by?

REFERENCES

Visit www.NonGrandparent.com
for click-able links.

Chapter 2

Merriam Webster Dictionary. (2024). *Grandparent.*
https://www.merriam-webster.com/dictionary/
grandparent

Cambridge English Dictionary. (2024). *Grandparent.*
https://dictionary.cambridge.org/us/dictionary/
english/grandparent

American Association of Retired Persons. (n.d.). *A living
legacy: How Ethel Percy Andrus changed America.*
https://www.aarp.org/about-aarp/history/

Lampkin, C. (2012). *Insights and spending habits of
modern grandparents.*
https://www.aarp.org/research/topics/life/info-
2014/grandparenting-survey.html

David, P., & Kakulla, B. (2019). 2018 *Grandparents Today
National Survey: General Population Report.*
Washington, DC: AARP Research.
https://doi.org/10.26419/res.00289.001

MetLife Mature Market Institute and Generations United. (2012). *Grandparents investing in grandchildren study.* https://www.healthworkscollective.com/wp-content/uploads/2012/12/MMIGrandparentsStudy_WEB.pdf

Considerable.com Editors. (2009). *Surprising facts about grandparents: We reveal how today's grandparents are defying stereotypes.* https://web.archive.org/web/20200919025625/ https://www.considerable.com/life/family/ surprising-facts-about-grandparents/

Chapter 3

LaFlamme, L. (n.d.). *Alex Trebek on his health, family and legacy.* [Video]. YouTube. https://www.youtube.com/ watch?v=p6PByjRnmh4&t=1160s

Trebek, A. (2020). *The answer is....Reflections on my life.* New York: Simon and Schuster.

Centers for Disease Control and Prevention. (2021a) *Infertility FAQs.* https://www.cdc.gov/reproductive-health/infertility-faq/index.html

Nugent, C., & Chandra, A. (2024). Infertility and impaired fecundity in women and men in the United States, 2015-2019. *National Health Statistics Reports, Number 202*: April 24, 2024. United States Department of Health and Human Services and Centers for Disease Control and Prevention National Center for Health Statistics. https://www.cdc.gov/nchs/data/nhsr/nhsr202.pdf

March of Dimes. (October, 2024). *Miscarriage.*
    https://www.marchofdimes.org/find-support/
    topics/miscarriage-loss-grief/miscarriage

United States National Library of Medicine. (2022).
    Medline Plus: Miscarriage.
    https://medlineplus.gov/ency/article/001488.htm

United States National Library of Medicine. (2021).
    Medline Plus: Stillbirth.
    https://medlineplus.gov/stillbirth.html

Center for Disease Control and Prevention. (2024b). *Data
    and statistics on stillbirth.*
    https://www.cdc.gov/stillbirth/data-research/index.
    html

Center for Disease Control and Prevention. (2024c). *Data
    and Statistics for SUID and SIDS.*
    https://www.cdc.gov/sudden-infant-death/data-
    research/data/index.html

March of Dimes. (October, 2024). *Neonatal death.*
    https://www.marchofdimes.org/find-support/
    topics/miscarriage-loss-grief/neonatal-death

Bennett, N. (2005). *Forgotten tears: A grandmother's
    journey through grief.* BookLocker.com, Inc.

Cambridge English Dictionary. (2024). *Childlessness.*
    https://dictionary.cambridge.org/us/dictionary/
    english/childlessness

Schondelmyer, E. (2017). *More adults living without
    children: Fewer married households and more
    living alone.*
    http://www.census.gov/library/stories/2017/08/
    more-adults-living-without-children.html

Tavernise, S., Miller, C., Bui, Q., & Gebeloff, R. (2021). Why more American women are delaying motherhood. *The New York Times.* https://www.nytimes.com/2021/06/16/us/declining-birthrate-motherhood.html

Williams Institute. (n.d.). *Transgender people.* https://williamsinstitute.law.ucla.edu/subpopulations/transgender-people/

Hamilton, B.E., Martin, J.A., & Osterman, M.J.K. (2022). *Births: Provisional data for 2021: Vital Statistics Rapid Release.* National Center for Health Statistics. https://www.cdc.gov/nchs/data/vsrr/vsrr020.pdf

Pillemer, K. (2020). *Fault lines: Fractured families and how to mend them.* New York, Avery Publishers.

Pew Research Center. (2024). *The American family today.* Washington, DC. https://www.pewresearch.org/social-trends/2015/12/17/1-the-american-family-today/

Livingston, G. (2018). *The changing profile of unmarried parents.* Pew Research Center. Washington, DC. https://www.pewresearch.org/social-trends/wp-content/uploads/sites/3/2018/04/Unmarried-Parents-Full-Report-PDF.pdf

Chapter 5

Weiss, R. S. (2008). The nature and causes of grief. In M. S. Stroebe, R. O. Hansson, H. Schut, & W. Stroebe (Eds.), *Handbook of bereavement research and practice: Advances in theory and intervention* (pp. 29–44). American Psychological Association. https://doi.org/10.1037/14498-002

American Psychological Association. (2024). *Definition of grief*. Washington DC.
https://dictionary.apa.org/grief

Cleveland Clinic. (2023). Grief. *Overview: What is grief?*
https://my.clevelandclinic.org/health/diseases/24787-grief

Worden, J.W. (2008). *Grief counseling and grief therapy: A handbook for the mental health practitioner (4th ed.)*. New York: Springer.

Adikew, M. (2020). *What is grief counseling? How does it help?*
https://www.talkspace.com/blog/grief-counseling-therapy-definition-what-is/

Open to Hope Foundation. (2017). *The 3 R's of processing grief*. [Video]. YouTube.
https://www.youtube.com/watch?v=G7Lm-Fo2UGw

Wolfelt, A. (n.d.). *Grief and mourning basics*.
https://www.centerforloss.com/grief/grief-mourning-basics/

Carter-Lome, M. (2024). The evolution of mourning wear. *The Journal of Antiques and Collectibles*.
https://journalofantiques.com/features/the-evolution-of-mourning-wear/

illume Editorial Team. (2023). *Grief in different cultures and religions*.
https://illumeapps.com/griefworks-blog/grief-in-different-cultures-and-religions/

National Cancer Institute. (2024). *Grief, bereavement, and loss: Patient version*.
https://www.cancer.gov/about-cancer/advanced-cancer/caregivers/planning/bereavement-pdq

National Institutes of Health. (2021). *Depression. U.S. Department of Health and Human Services, National Institutes of Health, NIH Publication No. 21-MH-8079.* https://www.nimh.nih.gov/health/publications/depression/index.shtml

Substance Abuse Mental Health Services Administration. (n.d.). *National suicide prevention lifeline.* Rockville, MD. https://suicidepreventionlifeline.org/

Chapter 6

Kübler-Ross, E. (1969). *On death and dying.* New York: Macmillan.

Kübler-Ross, E., & Kessler, D. (2005). *On grief and grieving: Finding the meaning of grief through the five stages of loss.* New York: Scribner.

Kübler-Ross, E., & Kessler, D. (n.d.) *On grief and grieving: Five stages of grief (condensed version).* https://grief.com/images/pdf/5%20Stages%20of%20Grief.pdf

Hall, C. (2011). Beyond Kubler-Ross: Recent developments in our understanding of grief and bereavement. *InPsych: The Bulletin of the Australian Psychological Society Ltd, 33(6).* https://psychology.org.au/inpsych/2011/dec

Garcia, C. (February 20, 2014). *Transformed, healed, restored blog.* http://transformedhealedandrestored.blogspot.com/2014/02/grief-and-loss.html

Worden, J. W. (2018). *Grief counseling and grief therapy: A handbook for the mental health practitioner (5th ed.).* New York: Springer.

Our House Grief Support Center. (2022). *Worden's four tasks of mourning.* https://www.ourhouse-grief.org/grief-pages/grieving-adults/four-tasks-of-mourning/

Chapter 9

Ocean, L. (2024). *The history of yoga.* https://www.mindisthemaster.com/the-history-of-yoga/#

Watson, S. (2022). Yoga: How it works. *WebMD.* https://www.webmd.com/fitness-exercise/a-z/yoga-workouts

American Osteopathic Association. (2024). *The benefits of yoga: Maintaining a regular yoga practice can provide both physical and mental health benefits.* https://osteopathic.org/benefits-of-yoga/

Yoga Home. (n.d.). *About Yoga Home: Meet our team: Kerri Hanlon* https://ouryogahome.com/team/

Pascoe, M., de Manincor, M., Tseberja, J., Hallgren, M., Baldwin, P., & Parker, A. (2001). Psychobiological mechanisms underlying the mood benefits of meditation: A narrative review, *Comprehensive Psychoneuroendocrinology, 6.* https://doi.org/10.1016/j.cpnec.2021.100037.

Allen, C. (2020). The potential health benefits of meditation. *American College of Sports Medicine's Health & Fitness Journal, 24, (6),* 28-32. https://doi: 10.1249/FIT.0000000000000624.

Stang, H. (2018). *Can meditation help with grief?*
https://mindfulnessandgrief.com/can-meditation-
help-with-grief/

Stang, H. (2021). *Guided meditation for grief and sadness.*
https://mindfulnessandgrief.com/meditation-for-
grief-and-sadness/

United States Department of Agriculture and United States
Department of Health and Human Services. (n.d.).
*2020-2050 Dietary Guidelines for Americans (9th
ed.).*
https://www.dietaryguidelines.gov/resources/2020-
2025-dietary-guidelines-online-materials/top-10-
things-you-need-know-about-dietary

Solan, M. (2023). How much sleep do you actually need?
Sleep quality counts as much as hours logged.
Harvard Health Publishing.
https://www.health.harvard.edu/blog/how-much-
sleep-do-you-actually-need-202310302986

Zohu, E. (2023). In Solan, M. How much sleep do you
actually need? Sleep quality counts as much as
hours logged. *Harvard Health Publishing.*
https://www.health.harvard.edu/blog/how-much-
sleep-do-you-actually-need-202310302986

Newsom, R., & Singh, A. (2024). *Blue light: What it is and
how it affects sleep.* The Sleep Foundation.
https://www.sleepfoundation.org/bedroom-
environment/blue-light

Christensen, M.A., Bettencourt. L., Kaye, L., Moturu, S.T., Nguyen, K.T., Olgin, J.E., Pletcher, M.J., & Marcus, G.M. (2016). Direct measurements of smartphone screen-time: Relationships with demographics and sleep. *PLoS One, 9 (11)*, e0165331. https://www.ncbi.nlm.nih.gov/pmc/articles/PMC5102460/

Harvard Health Publishing. (2022). *Blue light has a dark side.* https://www.health.harvard.edu/staying-healthy/blue-light-has-a-dark-side

Mayo Clinic. (2024). *Sleep aids: Understand options sold without a prescription.* https://www.mayoclinic.org/healthy-lifestyle/adult-health/in-depth/sleep-aids/art-20047860

Cleveland Clinic. (2023, April 21). What to expect as a parent of a rainbow baby. *Cleveland Clinic Health Essentials.* https://www.google.com/search?client=firefox-b-1-d&q=what+is+a+rainbow+baby

ABOUT THE AUTHOR

Dr. Mary Ellen T. Miller is a Registered Nurse who holds national board certification in Public Health Nursing. She has over thirty years' experience as a nurse educator, retiring from DeSales University as an Associate Professor. From 2008 to 2023, she directed an interprofessional internship for health professions students, the Lehigh Valley Affiliate of *Bridging the Gaps*. Dr. Miller has authored nursing textbook chapters and articles in peer reviewed professional journals. She co-authored several federal, state, and local grant applications to support student initiatives. She continues to do presentations at national, regional, and local professional conferences.

Mary Ellen has been married to her best friend, Drew, for over four decades, and they are enjoying their retirement years in the mountains of Pennsylvania. She enjoys gardening and time with her fur-baby, family, and friends. Mary Ellen's proudest accomplishment is, along with Drew, raising two daughters, Ashley and Amanda, who are compassionate women and committed to social justice.

Send your comments and/or suggestions to the author at:
nursemaryellen1977@gmail.com

www.NonGrandparent.com

www.ingramcontent.com/pod-product-compliance
Lightning Source LLC
Chambersburg PA
CBHW061149120626
46546CB00005B/1979